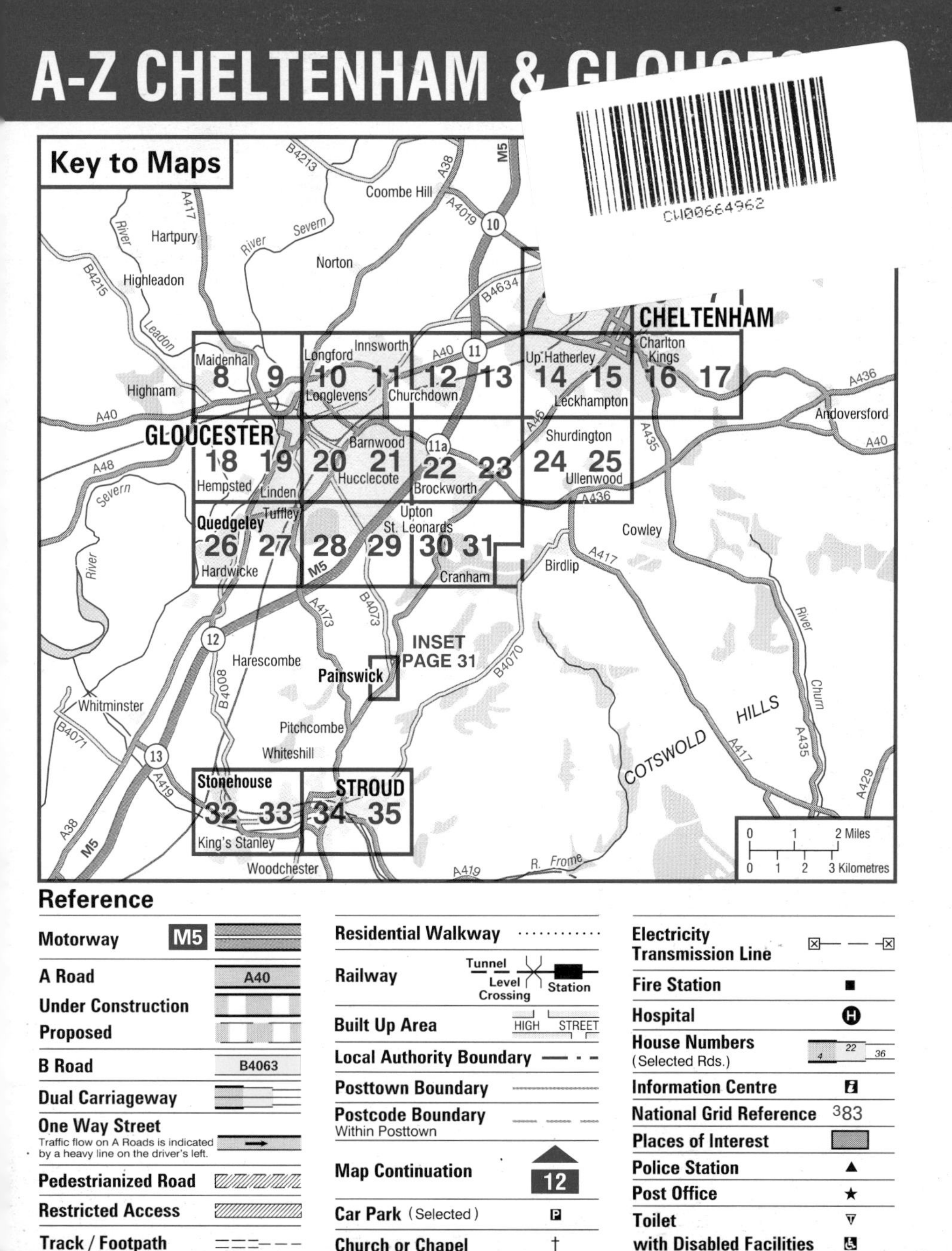

Scale 4 inches (10.16 cm) to 1 mile
1:15,840 6.31 cm to 1 km

0 ¼ ½ Mile
0 250 500 750 Metres 1 Kilometre

Geographers' A-Z Map Company Ltd.

Head Office :
Fairfield Road, Borough Green, Sevenoaks, Kent TN15 8PP
Tel: 01732 781000
Showrooms :
44 Gray's Inn Road, London WC1X 8HX
Tel: 020 7440 9500

1998 EDITION 2 1999 EDITION 2A (part revision)

2
A
B
C
D
94
395
28
27
26
25
1
2
3
4
5
6
Glebe Farm
Court Farm
STOKE ORCHARD ROAD
Wingmoor Lodge
The Park
Wingmoor Farm
MALVERN VIEW BUSINESS PARK
Depot
Irish Butts
Pav.
Rugby Ground
STELLA WY.
HUXLEY WY.
HAYFIELDS
LITTLE ACORNS
WAY
BISHOP'S CLEEVE BY-PASS
A435
LAKE HOUSE PARK
JARDINE DR.
CHILTERN AV.
Cleeve Lake Ct.
VOXWELL
TEWKE
Offices
Bishop's Cleeve
Lower Farm
MEADOW
Southam Field Farm
MEADOW LEA
MEADOWAY
BREGAWN CL.
ALVERTON DR.
CLEEVE BUSINESS PARK
Engineering Works
HYDE
Chelt
Brockhampton
Lower Farm
Upper Farm
St Magdalene's Farm
Longacre Farm
BROCKHAMPTON LANE
Sewage Works
BROOK LANE
Nursery
GL51
Hyde Farm
GL50
BROCKHAMPTON
Home Farm
CHELTENHAM
HYDE ROAD
A435
EVESHAM
Cotteswold
THE FIRS
GOOSE
QUAT
Swindon
DARK LANE
STANTONS DR.
HULBERT CL.
RIVELANDS RD.
Pav.
Sports Ground
Swindon Village Prim. Sch.
Tennis Courts
DEAKIN CL.
LANE
SMYTHE
RECTORY LA.
CHURCH
Swindon Manor
MANOR CT.
Swindon Hall
Playing Field
5

E
F
G
H
3
96
97
28
27
26
25
1
2
3
4
5
6
Woodmancote
Southam
GL52
Bishop's Cleeve Prim. Sch.
Cleeve School
Woodmancote Prim. Sch.
Recreation Ground
Playing Field
Sports Ground
Public Open Space
Play. Fld.
Home Farm
Mills
Library
Orchard House
The Green
Rectory Ct.
Nurseries
Yew Tree Farm
Box Farm
Poplar Farm
Folly Farm
Gambles Farm
Woodmancote Farm
Southam Paddocks
Haymes Farm
Cedar Farm
The Bungalow
Kayte Farm
Kayte Cottages
Manor Farm
Hotel
Riding School
CHELTENHAM RACECOURSE
Southam Bridge
OXBUTTS PARK
STATION ROAD
CHURCH ROAD
TWO HEDGES ROAD
PRIORY LANE
LONGLANDS ROAD
BUSHCOMBE LANE
STOCKWELL LANE
GAMBLES LANE
NEW ROAD
BUTT'S LANE
KAYTE LANE
SOUTHAM LANE
SOUTHAM ROAD
CHELTENHAM ROAD
EVESHAM ROAD
HYDE BROOK
B4632
BENTLEY LANE
SUNSET LA.
ASHLEIGH LA.
HAYMES RD.
HAYMES DR.
DELABERE ROAD
PAGETS ROAD
ELLENBOROUGH RD.
MORETON CL.
SUNNYCROFT CL.
POTTERS FIELD ROAD
APPLE TREE CL.
CRANFORD CL.
DENHAM CL.
PEAR TREE CL.
GREEN LORDS
HILLSIDE CL.
HILLSIDE GDNS.
BEVERLEY GDNS.
AESOPS ORCHARD
BUSHCOMBE CL.
GREENWAY
CROWFIELD
CHAPEL LA.
POPLAR DR.
MEADE-KING GRO.
COOMBE MEADE
EAST GABLE
BRITANNIA WAY
CELANDINE BK.
DEWEY CL.
COTSWOLD VW.
WOODMANCOTE VALE
THE ROWANS
WHITEHOUSE WAY
KEEPERS MDW.
COWSLIP MDW.
THATCHERS END
PEAKSTILE PIECE
KEMPSFORD ACRE
MILLHAM ROAD
OXMEAD CL.
LONGLANDS CL.
PINE BANK
WARD CL.
BIRCHFIELD RD.
WITHYFIELD RD.
ASHFIELD CL.
OAKFIELD RD.
FIELDGATE RD.
CHURCHFIELDS
PECKED LANE
SCHOOL RD.
TOBYFIELD RD.
TOBYFIELD CL.
HUNTSMANS CL.
LEARS DR.
BISHOPS CL.
BISHOPS DRIVE
BISHOPS DR.
WOODMANS WY.
DEAN'S WY.
HEMMING WY.
COURTIERS DR.
MINETTS AV.
ST. MICHAELS AV.
MEADS CL.
HYATTS WY.
JESSON RD.
LINWORTH RD.
DALE WLK.
CLEEVE CL.
HARPFIELD CL.
CROWN DR.
GRANGER CL.
DENLEY CL.
KAYTE CL.
GILDER RD.
HOLDER RD.
READ WY.
READ WAY
CHANDLER RD.
KINGSWOOD CL.
ORCHARD RD
STATION ROAD
GILDERS PADDOCK
CHURCH APP.
SELBOURNE RD.
SANDOWN
NOTTINGHAM RD.
BERWICK RD.
WELLBROOK RD.
HARDY ROAD
HERTFORD RD.
SHIPWAY CT.
FOSTER CL.
GOTHERINGTON LA.
OLD ACRE DRIVE
OLD ACRE DR.
BOOTENHAY RD.
CARES CL.
OWLS END
BARKER'S LEYS
RATCLIFF LAWNS
THE CLOSE
SCHOOL LA.
OLD SCHOOL
Gravel Wk.
ORIEL SCHOOL DR.
MURRAY CL.
ROBERTS CL.
STREAMSIDE
6

4
A
B
C
D
92
93
25
24
23
22
1
2
3
4
5
6
TEWKESBURY
GL51
Cheltenham
TEWKESBURY ROAD A4019
The Orchard
Uckington Farm
Pigeon House Farm
COOKS LA.
Manor Farm
MOAT
The Green
LANE
Newhouse Farm
Old Hall
Moat
Moat House
Uckington
River Chelt
HOMECROFT DRI.
Sports Gnd. & Club
Bar Bridge
Warehouses
Superstore
GALLAGHER RETAIL PK.
Swindon Farm
Industrial Estate
Swindon Manor
MANOR ROAD
DOG BARK LANE
RUNNINGS
MACKENZIE WY.
RUTHERFORD WY.
MALMESBURY RD.
KINGSDITCH RETAIL PK.
KINGSDITCH
Piggery
Pilgrove Bridge
OLD B4634 GLOUCESTER ROAD
HAYDEN RD.
B4634
COPPICE GATE
RIVER LEYS
BLAISDON WY.
WILLIAM GOUGH CL.
ATTWOOD CL.
Bedlam Farm
Orchard Park
WALDRIST CL.
GLYNBRIDGE GARDENS
RIVERVIEW WY.
PILGROVE WY.
GRIST MILL CL.
WHEATLAND DR.
HAZLEDEAN RD.
SOMERGATE RD.
BARNETT CL.
SEABRIGHT CL.
GRENADIER RD.
BODHAM RD.
Shop. Cen.
GRAVINEY CT.
PETER PENNELL CL.
Cheltenham Kingsmead School
Playing Field
Arle House
Public Open Space
KINGSMEAD CLO.
Warehouse
Works
Arle
A4013
KINGSMEAD IND. EST.
Training Centre
BROOK RD.
MOORS
Brooklyn Ct.
BROOKLYN GARDENS
HOPE ORCHARD
Play. Fld.
Arthur Dye Prim. Sch.
SPRINGBANK ROAD
CARROL GR.
Woodbine Cottage
DUNBAR CL.
LEINSTER CL.
SOLWAY ROAD
BEAUMONT ROAD
HESTER'S WAY
WELCH ROAD
ISMAY RD.
DILL AV.
LIPSON RD.
Hesters Way Jun. & Inf. Sch.
ASHLANDS ROAD
ASHLANDS CL.
KINGSMEAD AV.
REDGROVE RD.
ELIZABETH WAY
PENNSYLVANIA AV.
MARCHANT CL.
LEE CL.
ARLE RD.
New Zealand Ho.
Telford Ho.
RUSSET RD.
ORCHARD AVENUE
BRAMLEY RD.
TANNER'S RD.
ALSTONE AV.
Sports Gnd.
ATHERSTONE CL.
HARTBY CL.
HENLEY ROAD
DUNSTER CL.
WENTWORTH CL.
STANLEY RD.
FALKLAND PL.
OLDBURY RD.
BARBRIDGE RD.
LECHMERE RD.
Scott Ho.
Edward Wilson House
Montreal Ho.
Canada Ho.
Quebec Ho.
HAWTHORN RD.
BLENHEIM SQ.
Mkt.
NETHERWOOD CL.
Sandfields
Playing Field
Pate's Mixed Grammar School (Upper)
PRINCESS ELIZABETH WAY
Hester's Way
Health Centre
NEWTON RD.
NEWTON CL.
DOWTY RD.
Rowanfield Jun. & Inf. Schs.
King George V Playing Field
CORNWALL AV.
Fiddler's Green
ASTON GR.
Rushworth Ho.
MARSLAND RD.
WINTERBOTHAM RD.
Public Open Space
Royal Ct.
TERRY
Primary School
LEWIS RD.
SEACOMBE RD.
Pakistan Ho.
India Ho.
ST. AIDAN'S CL.
CORONATION SQ.
Sochi Ct.
BROOKLYN RD.
Rowanfield
SOMERSET AV.
BUCKINGHAM AV.
DORSET AV.
BEDFORD AV.
Bishop Ct.
ESSEX AV.
PARKBURY CL.
SUSSEX AV.
EDINBURGH PL.
ALDER CT.
FIDDLER'S GREEN
KEMPTON GROVE
Elm Fm.
CAMBERWELL RD.
Play Area
Pate's Mixed Grammar Sch. (Lower)
Evington Ct.
EVINGTON RD.
AMBERLEY RD.
Liby.
Ten. Cts.
Comm. Cen.
Youth Cen.
St. Mark's Rec. Grd.
Works
SURREY AV.
CAMBRIDGE AV.
NORFOLK AV.
SHAKESPEARE ROAD
Hesters Way Park
Monkscroft Jun. & Inf. Sch.
TENNYSON RD.
DEVON AV.
CUMBERLAND CR.
Sunningend Works
LANSDOWN INDUSTRIAL ESTATE
SHELLEY AV.
St. Mark's
BYRON RD.
LIBERTUS RD.
ROWANFIELD RD.
GRIMWADE CL.
ROMAN RD.
Sch.
Government Communications H. Q. (Benhill)
BISHOPSTONE CL.
PITMAN RD.
COWPER RD.
WORDSWORTH AV.
KIPLING RD.
SPENSER AV.
HILLFIELD
The Granleys
Hillfield
B4633
QUEEN'S RD.
KINGSTON DR.
EDENDALE
DARWIN CL.
CASTLEMAINE DR.
GLOUCESTER ROAD A40
Subway
BENHALL GDS.
KINGSLEY GDS.
MILTON RD.
OLDFIELD CR.
CAMPDEN RD.
MISERDEN RD.
FARMINGTON RD.
GRIFFITHS AV.
CHURCH RD.
CHELTENHAM SPA
GLOUCESTER RD.
QUEEN'S CT.
Glencairn
14

E
F
G
H
5
2
94
395
1
2
3
4
5
6
9
15
24
22
Swindon Village Prim. Sch.
Tennis Courts
Swindon Hall
Playing Field
Swindon
Pav.
Bowling Alley
Industrial Estate
Swindon Bridge
Works
Maud's Elm
Tewkesbury Bridge
Depot
Gas Works
Superstore
St. Peter's
The Folley (Cheltenham & Gloucester Coll. Grd.)
Cleeve View Inf. Sch.
Elmfield County Jun. Sch.
Morality Farm
Guestriss Cotts.
Wymans Court
Hunting Butts
The Paddocks
Race Course Car Park
Hall of Fame
Grand Stand
Winning Posts
CHELTENHAM RACECOURSE
Rosehill
Cleevemont
THE SPINNEY
Pittville Pump Room (Spa)
Ellerslie
Pittville School
Pittville Lake
Pittville
APPROACH GOLF COURSE
Marle Hill
CHELTENHAM RECN. CENTRE
Marle Hill Lake
PITTVILLE PARK
Prince of Wales Stadm
Swim. Pool
Tennis Cts
Recreation Ground
Sports Ground
Hardwick Building
St. Paul's
Francis Close Hall
GL50
Brewery
Lib. & Mus.
Mem. Gdns.
Gloucestershire Coll. of Art & Tech.
Playing Field
CHELTENHAM
Fulton House
Benefits Off.
Warehouse
Swimming Bath
Glenlee
Tennis Cts.
Games Ct.
Playing Field
Airthrie Sch.
Overton Park
Abbeyholme
Bayshill
Ladies Coll.
The Quadrangle Imperial Gdns.
T.H.
Muni. Offs.
Everyman Th.
Regent Arcade
County Court
Beechwood The Pl. Arcade
Lansdown
Montpellier
SANDFORD PK. TRAD. EST.
EVESHAM ROAD
A435
NEW BARN LANE
B4075
SWINDON ROAD
A4019
HIGH ST.
ST. MARGARET'S RD.
FAIRVIEW RD.
ST. JOHN'S AV.
A46
PROMENADE
B4633
HYDE ROAD
WYMANS
WINDYRIDGE
PRESTBURY
PITTVILLE CIRCUS
HEWLETT RD.
LONDON ROAD
ST. GEORGES
MALVERN
PARABOLA

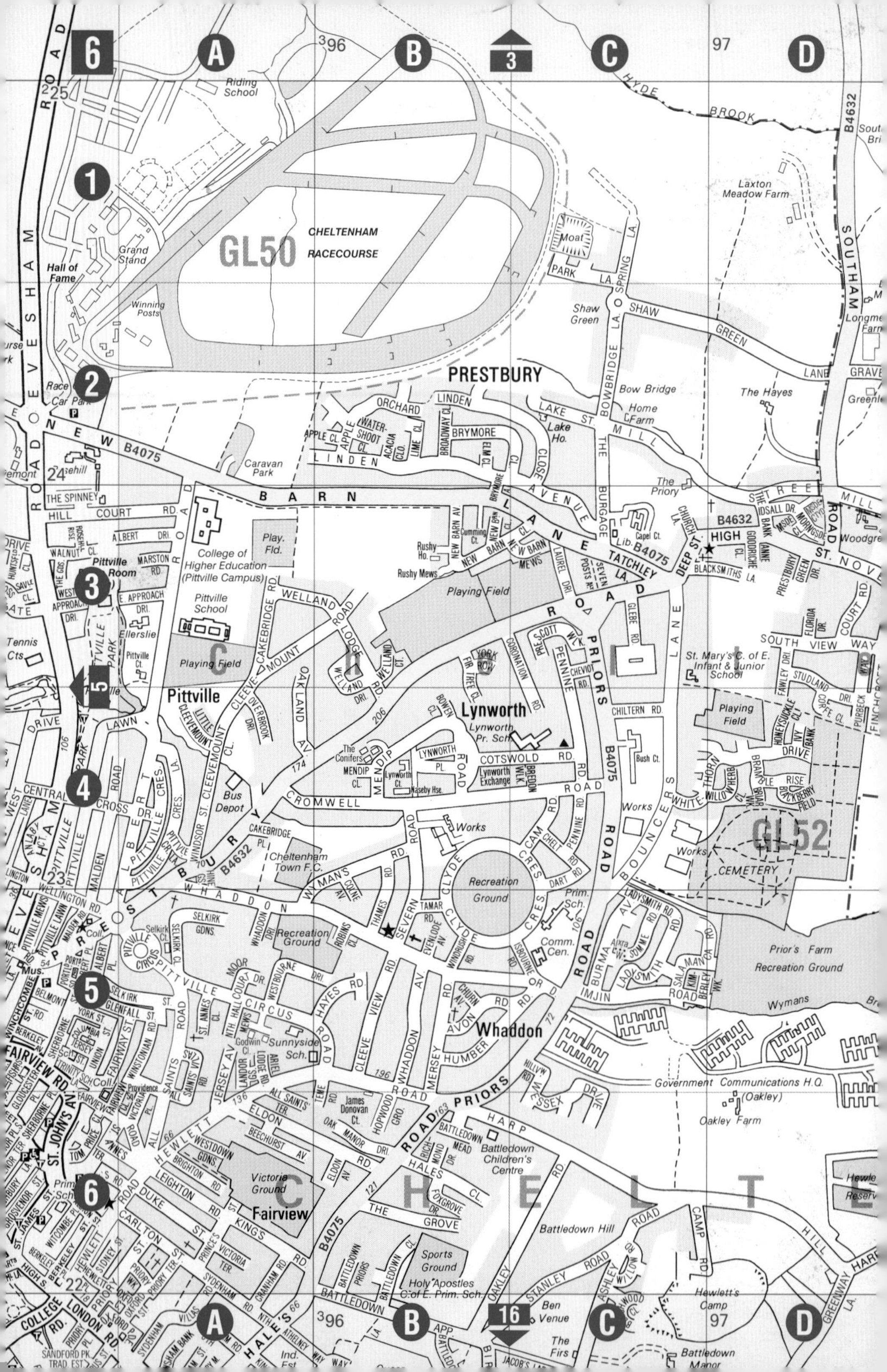

6
A
B
C
D
3
396
97
Riding School
CHELTENHAM RACECOURSE
GL50
Grand Stand
Hall of Fame
Winning Posts
Race Car Park
PRESTBURY
HYDE BROOK
B4632
Laxton Meadow Farm
SOUTHAM
Moat
PARK LA.
SPRING LA.
Shaw Green
SHAW GREEN LANE
BOWBRIDGE LA.
Bow Bridge
Home Farm
The Hayes
Lake Ho.
LAKE ST.
MILL
The Priory
NEW B4075
BARN LANE
Caravan Park
ORCHARD
LINDEN
BRYMORE
APPLE CL.
ACACIA CLO.
LIME CL.
BROADWAY CL.
ELM CL.
CLOSE
AVENUE
THE BURGAGE
HIGH
DEEP ST.
CHURCH LA.
B4075
TATCHLEY LA.
Lib.
Capel Ct.
BLACKSMITHS LA.
GOODRICHE CL.
PRESTBURY GREEN DR.
COURT RD.
FLORIDA DR.
SOUTH VIEW WAY
St. Mary's C. of E. Infant & Junior School
Playing Field
STUDLAND DRI.
FAWLEY DRI.
PURBECK
HONEYSUCKLE CL.
IVY BANK
DRIVE
RISE
WHITETHORN
BOUNCERS LANE
GL52
CEMETERY
Works
Prior's Farm Recreation Ground
Wymans
Government Communications H.Q. (Oakley)
Oakley Farm
THE SPINNEY
HILL COURT RD.
ALBERT DRI.
MARSTON RD.
WALNUT
Pittville Pump Room
College of Higher Education (Pittville Campus)
Play. Fld.
Pittville School
Playing Field
Rushy Ho.
Rushy Mews
NEW BARN AV.
Cumming Ct.
NEW BARN MEWS
ROAD
PRIORS ROAD
LAUREL DRI.
SEVEN POSTS AV.
GLEBE RD.
Pittville
Tennis Cts.
Ellerslie
Pittville Ct.
WELLAND
LODGE
OAKLAND AV.
CAKEBRIDGE RD.
MOUNT
CLEEVEMOUNT CL.
OVERBROOK DRI.
LITTLE CLEEVEMOUNT
YORK ROW
FIR TREE CL.
CORONATION
PENNINE
CHEVIOT RD.
PRESCOTT WK.
Lynworth
Lynworth Pr. Sch.
BOWEN CL.
MENDIP
The Conifers
LYNWORTH PL.
COTSWOLD RD.
Lynworth Exchange
BREDON WK.
CHILTERN RD.
Bush Ct.
CROMWELL
Bus Depot
WINDSOR ST.
CLEEVEMOUNT
PITTVILLE CRES.
PITTVILLE LAWN
WEST
CENTRAL
CROSS DR.
ALBERT
MALDEN
CAKEBRIDGE PL.
PRESTBURY B4632
Cheltenham Town F.C.
WYMAN'S RD.
WHADDON
Recreation Ground
CLYDE CRES.
CAM
CHELT
PENNINE
DART RD.
Prim. Sch.
Comm. Cen.
LADYSMITH RD.
BURMA AV.
SOMME
SALAMANCA RD.
KIMBERLEY WK.
IMJIN ROAD
WELLINGTON RD.
PITTVILLE CIRCUS
SELKIRK GDNS.
Recreation Ground
ROBINS CL.
THAMES RD.
COLNE AV.
SEVERN
TAMAR RD.
EVENLODE AV.
ISBOURNE RD.
WINDRUSH RD.
Mus.
SELKIRK ST.
GLENFALL ST.
MOOR COURT DR.
WESTBOURNE DRI.
HAYES RD.
CLEEVE VIEW RD.
WHADDON AV.
MERSEY RD.
CHURN AV.
AVON
Whaddon
HUMBER
HILLVIEW RD.
WESSEX DRIVE
Sunnyside Sch.
ST. ANNES RD.
FAIRVIEW RD.
ST. JOHN'S AV.
WINSTONIAN RD.
JERSEY AV.
ALL SAINTS' RD.
ALL SAINTS' TER.
ELDON
James Donovan Ct.
HOPWOOD GRO.
PRIORS ROAD
HARP
BATTLEDOWN MEAD
Battledown Children's Centre
RICHMOND DR.
HALES CL.
FOXGROVE DR.
THE GROVE
OAK MANOR DRI.
BEECHURST AV.
HEWLETT
WESTDOWN GDNS.
BRIGHTON RD.
LEIGHTON RD.
DUKE
Victoria Ground
Fairview
KINGS
CARLTON ST.
PRINCE'S
VICTORIA TER.
GRANHAM RD.
SYDENHAM
B4075
BATTLEDOWN PRIORS
BATTLEDOWN CL.
Sports Ground
Holy Apostles C. of E. Prim. Sch.
OAKLEY
Battledown Hill
STANLEY ROAD
ASHLEY RD.
WILLOW RD.
CAMP RD.
Hewlett's Camp
HILL
GREENWAY LA.
Ben Venue
The Firs
Battledown Manor
16
BATTLEDOWN
HALE'S
Ind. Est.
LONDON RD.
COLLEGE RD.
SANDFORD PK TRAD. EST.
Prim. Sch.
ST. JAMES
22
23
24
25
1
2
3
4
5
6
CHELTENHAM

7
E
F
G
H
98
99
25
24
23
22
1
2
3
4
5
6
Queen's Wood
TEWKESBURY
White's Barn
LANE
Knoll Hill House
Queenwood Grove
GROVE
Brookfield Farm
Prestbury Hill
MILL
Moss Bank Farm
Upper Hill Farm
The Pitch
PIT
QUEENWOOD
The Mill
Badgers Mount Farm
UPPER
LANE
Whitehill
Brookfield House
LANE
Burnside
NOVERTON AV.
LANE
Drake's Farm
Noverton Farm
MUSCROFT RD.
ROAD
PICCADILLY WY.
Noverton
CLEEVE CLOUD LA.
SISTERS
ROBERTS
BUTTERCROSS LA.
WEST-WOOD LA.
nham
Quarries (dis.)
Piccadilly Farm
GL54
The Hewletts
HILL
Lower Hewletts Farm
AGGS
NHAM
Northfield Farm
Reservoir (covered)
COTSWOLD
MILL LANE
LANE
Lodge
Waterfall
E
98
F
17
G
99
H

A
B
C
D
380
81
22
21
220
19
1
2
3
4
5
6
Hill View
Parva Dene
Old Vicarage
A417
OLD ROAD
CHURCH ROAD
THE STEADINGS BUSINESS CENTRE
Vicarage
Bell House Farm
Hall
CHURCH RISE
BLACKSMITHS LA.
ORCHARD WY.
Football Field
PERSH LA.
PERSH WAY
PERSH LANE
ST. GILES CT.
THE RIDINGS
STANLEIGH TER.
Ivydene
Rectory Farm
Maisemore
Seapiece Covert
Lassington Court
The Reddings
Lassington
LANE
T E W K E
Astman's Farm
Cuckoo Pen Brake
PERSH
Persh Farm Cottages
Persh Farm
GL2
Rectory
Lassington Hill
KNIGHTS RIDGE
LIMEKILN GROVE
PIPERS GRO.
MARY GRO.
THE RANGE
Maidenhall
Sch
WETHERLEIGH DR.
GORDON CL.
BRIMSOME
BARN GD.
MEADOW
MAIDENHALL
LASSINGTON
Lassington Wood Nature Reserve
The Green
NEWENT
Sewage Works
River Leadon
POPES MEADE
WILLIAMS ORCHARD
LITTLE ORCHARD
LANCARRIDGE
FARTHING CROFT
BEECH CL.
PARK BRAKE
TURNERS CL.
B4215
The Rectory
Church Lodge
Highnam
LASSINGTON LANE
Over Farm
Pope's Pool Cottages
Over
A40
Highnam Court
The Park
ROAD
G L O U C
The Lake
Boat House
Linton Lodge
Chepstow Lodge
Linton Farm
Subway
18
Pipers' Grove
Lower Parting

9
E
F
G
H
82
83
22
21
20
19
1
2
3
4
5
6
10
19
Linden Villa
White House
Abbot's Lodge
Goodeacres
Abloads Cottages
Weir
Lock House
Upper Parting
Tar Works
Cattle Grid
Base Lane Cottages
Wind Pump
Severnside
Coal Wharf
Abloads Court
RIVER SEVERN (EAST CHANNEL)
SANDHURST LANE
BASE LANE
Horn's Ditch
Broadboard Brook
Wotton Brook
Queens Dyke
Longford
MAISEMORE ROAD
RIVER SEVERN (WEST CHANNEL)
MAISEMORE HAM
ALNEY ISLAND
Meadow Cottage
Walham
Electricity Sub. Station
Caravan Site
Walham Green
WINFIELD HOSPITAL
Frog Castle
Frogcastle Farm
NORTHERN BY-PASS
A40
A417
GLOUCESTER
WALHAM LA
LAWRENCE WAY
Caravan Site
A40 GLOUCESTER ROAD
Over Bridge
Lower Walham
River Twyver (Dockham Ditch)
Playing Field
Ham Viaduct
Severnside Fm.
Archdeacon Meadow
Pump Ho. Bridge
Rugby Football Club
Warehouse
CATTLE MARKET INDUSTRIAL ESTATE
Cattle Market
Cattle Grid
MEAN HAM
TOWN HAM
Club House
St. Catherine's Viaduct
Electricity Switching Station
Pool Meadow
Boating Lake
Pitch & Putt Golf Course
WESTGATE LEISURE AREA
Sports Cen.
Tennis Cts.
King's Sch. Cricket Ground
Pav.
St. Catherine's Meadow Bri.
CAUSEWAY
OVER CAUSEWAY
GL1
RT HAM
Playing Field
Westgate Bridge
THE WESTGATE GALLERIA (SHOP. CEN.)
ST. OSWALDS RD.
PRIORY RD.
GOUDA WY.
Castle Meads Transforming Stn.
Play. Field
Cathedral
Fountain Sq.
St. Nicholas
STAMP'S MEADOW
TEWKESBURY RD.
PLOCK CT.
ORCHARD CT.
WESTFIELD TER.
FAIRMILE GDNS.
THE LIMES
HIGHBANK PARK
RIVERMEAD CLO
GAMBIER
PARRY
SANDHURST RD.
CHESMANN CT.
ESTCOURT RD.
Bowl. Grn.
Pav.
Ten. Ct.
Kingsholm
Sports Ground
HINTON ROAD
BIJOU CT.
The Willows
DENMARK
VINE TER
SEBERT ST.
Rec. Grd.
Kingsholm Prim. Sch.
UNION ST
SHERBORNE ST.
St. Mark's Ct.
Clapham Ct.
COLUMBIA CL.
OXFORD
KINGSHOLM COURT
KINGSHOLM SQUARE
DEAN'S TER
EDWY PDE
ST. MARK STREET
Gloucester R.F.C. Ground
DEAN'S WLK.
SERLO RD
Works
ST. CATHERINE
A430 KINGSHOLM
DEAN'S WAY
MERCIA ROAD
Depot
ST. OSWALDS
WORCESTER STREET
ALVIN STREET
County Records
Bus Depot
WESTEND PARADE
WEST END TER.
ALNEY TER
LEWIS

A
84
B
C
385
D
22
1
2
21
3
4
20
5
6
19
Court Cottages
The Hawthorns
A38
ROAD
Twigworth Lodge
War Memorial
Vicarage
Church Farm
Sch.
Brook
Broadboard Bridge
Broadboard
GL2
Horsbere Brook
Hatherley
Brook
Drymeadow Farm
Drymeadow Lodge
Longford Court
Longford Bridge
Chesterton Court
TEWKE
INNSWORTH TECHNOLOGY PARK
AUSTIN DRI.
Manor Farm
Sewage Purification Works
LEWIS AVE
SHERWOOD
GREEN
Longford
Wotton
Dyke
Brook
Field Farm
TEWKESBURY
LONGFORD
LONGFORD MEWS
Victoria Ct.
Playing Field
VICTORIA RD.
SIVELL
CRESCENTDALE
NORTHERN
A40
LACY CL.
DURAND CL.
WAY
A40
GLOUCESTER
BY-PASS
Finchmoor Mews
LONGFORD LA.
GLOUCESTER
FIRETHORNE CL.
FERNDALE CL.
FLEMING CL.
CRISPIN CL.
MANDEVILLE CL.
LITTLE WK
Mainard Sq.
STAMP'S MEADOW
TEWKESBURY R.
RD.
ALDERS GRN
WHITEBEAM CL.
HORNBEAM
MORTIMER RD.
MONTFORT RD.
BEAUMONT RD.
GIFFORD CL.
NORMANS
WINFIELD HOSPITAL
PLOCK CT.
G
L
O
U
C
MILFORD CL.
The Hawthorns Sch.
Chamwell School
Recreation Ground
Longford Sch.
SAXON CL.
GILBERT RD.
DANE CL.
SIMON RD.
Haydale Gdns.
BROOKLANDS
Frog Castle
ORCHARD
WESTFIELD TER
FAIRMILE GDNS.
Tennis Ct.
Sports Court
Playing Fields
OXSTALLS
BEECHCROFT
KENTON
DRIVE
CHARLTON WAY
THE LIMES
HIGHBANK PARK
Sports Ground
Longlevens
LANE
INNSWORTH
CHURCH RD
WEDGWOOD DRIVE
GAMBIER
GDNS.
Playing Field
REDLAND CLO.
RODNEY CLO.
ROAD
LONGLAND CT
LONGLAND GDNS.
CHAMWELLS WLK
CHURCH
ALDER CL.
WEDGWOOD
PARRY
Oxstalls Community School
Ten. Cts.
FLOWER
DRIVE
THE HEDGEROW
CHAMWELLS WLK
GLOUCESTER
BRADLEY CL.
ST. OSWALD'S RD.
SANDHURST RD
ESTCOURT
CL.
LAURA CL.
GARDEN WY.
GLEVUM CLO.
CHAMWELLS AV
WALLER CT.
GRASMERE
Lib.
Longlevens Jun. Sch.
Bowl. Grn.
Pav.
Ten. Ct.
Kingsholm
Sports Ground
HINTON ROAD
MALVERN ROAD
NORTH RD.
ESTCOURT CL.
Sports Ground
Pav.
Ten. Cts.
Playing Field
SOUTH CLO.
RYDAL ROAD
ROAD
WINDERMERE
KINGSHOLM COURT
KINGSHOLM SQUARE
BIJOU CT.
The Willows
COOKS ORCHARD
Playing Field
KENDAL RD.
THE TRIANGLE
DEAN'S TER
EDWY PDE
DENMARK
LANSDOWN
Hill Cotts.
A38
KESWICK CL.
WELLSPRINGS
VINE TER
ST. MARK STREET
High Sch.
Play. Field
SEABROKE RD.
OXSTALLS
CHELTENHAM
SEBERT ST.
JOHN WOOD'S Rec. Grd.
SHERBORNE
ROAD
ROAD
GL1
Ten. Cts.
B4063
COLEBRIDGE AV.
DEAN'S WLK.
SERLO RD
KINGSHOLM
SWAN ROAD
Kingsholm Prim. Sch.
St. Mark's Ct.
MICHAELMAS
Pav.
POSY LA.
Graham Gds
Cole Bri.
Works
WORCESTER ST.
UNION ST
HONYATT RD
Tudor Ct.
The Firs
Denmark Ct.
DENMARK ROAD DAY HOSP.
CHELTENHAM RD.
ESTCOURT
GRAFTON ROAD
MEREVALE
ROAD
CATHERINE
Clapham Ct.
ALEXANDRA RD.
HILLFIELD COURT RD.
Hillfield Gdns.
ELMBRIDGE
COLUMBIA STREET
OXFORD ROAD
HENRY ROAD
HEATHVILLE ROAD
RIVERSLEY ROAD
20
LONDON
Redcliffe College
KENILWORTH AV
ROAD
County Records
Clinic
Depot
Westminster

11
BRICKHAMPTON COURT GOLF COURSE
Club House
Brickhampton Court Farm
Water Reclamation Works
Innsworth Camp
Football Field
Innsworth
Innsworth House Farm
Pavilion
Sports Ground
Innsworth Jun. Sch.
Inf. Sch.
Larkfield Inf. Sch.
GL3
St. Mary's Prim. Sch.
Parklands
Parton Manor Inf. Sch.
Parton Manor Jun. Sch.
Play. Fld.
Rec Grd.
Liby.
Hall
Halfway Bridge
Government Buildings
Pirton Brake
Pirton Court
Elmbridge Court
Longlevens Inf.Sch.
Elm Bri.
Witcombe Bridge
Sir Thomas Rich's School
Tennis Cts.
Elmbridge
Playing Field
Pitch & Putt Golf Course
Recreation Ground
Well's Bridge
GL4
Zoons Court
Works
INNSWORTH LANE
FROG FURLONG LANE
CHELTENHAM ROAD
GOLDEN VALLEY BY-PASS
BARNWOOD A40/A417 LINK ROAD
PIRTON LANE
PARTON ROAD
B4063
A40
12
21

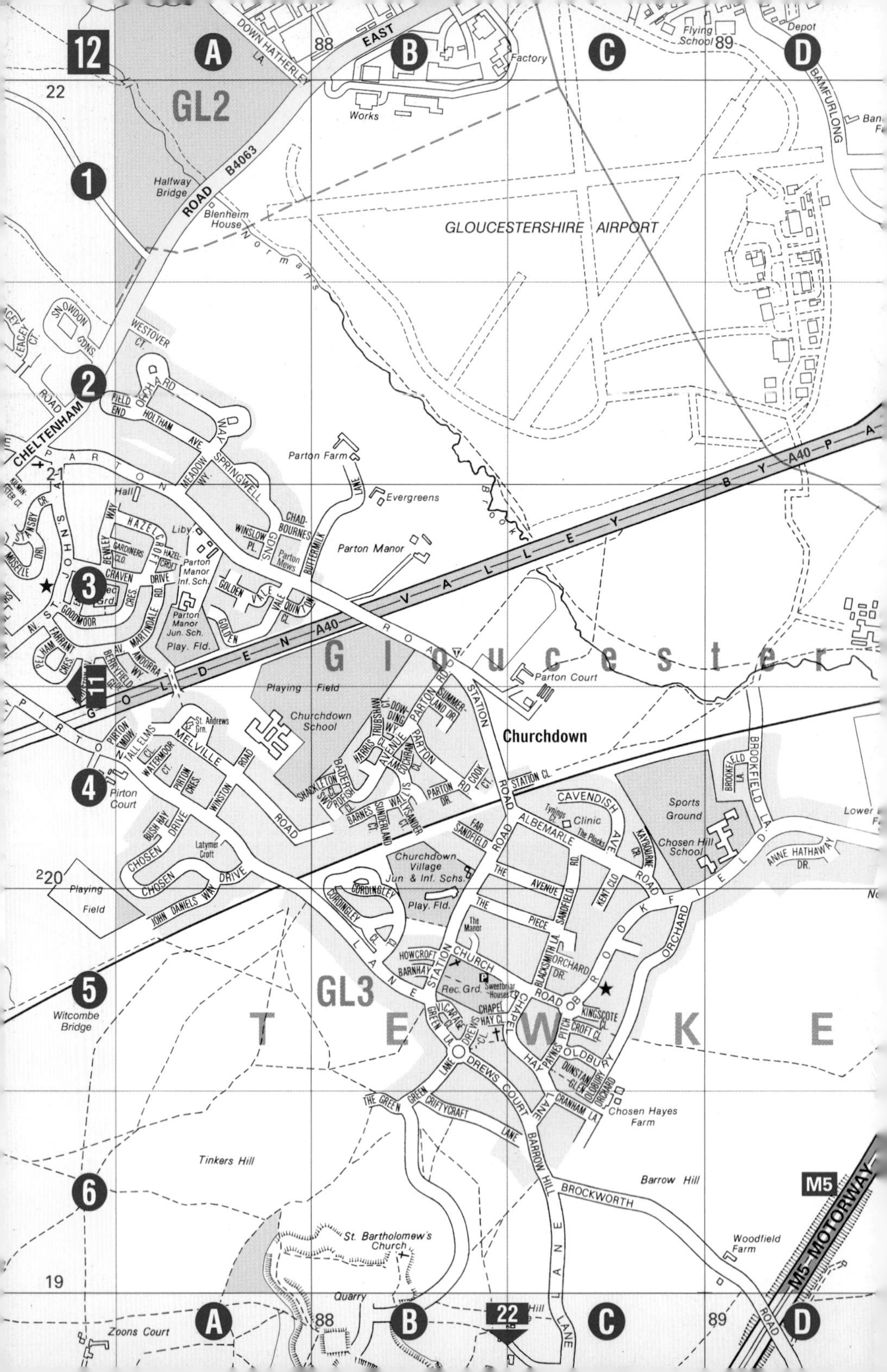
GL2
GLOUCESTERSHIRE AIRPORT
Flying School
Depot
Factory
Works
Halfway Bridge
Blenheim House
Normans Brook
B4063
ROAD
EAST
DOWN HATHERLEY LA.
BAMFURLONG
CHELTENHAM ROAD
SNOWDON GDNS.
LEACEY CT.
WESTOVER CT.
ORCHARD WAY
FIELD END
HOLTHAM AVE.
MEADOW WY.
SPRINGWELL
PARTON ROAD
CHADBOURNES
WINSLOW PL.
GDNS.
Parton Mews
BUTTERMILK LANE
Parton Farm
Evergreens
Parton Manor
Parton Manor Inf. Sch.
Parton Manor Jun. Sch.
Play. Fld.
Liby
Hall
HAZEL CROFT
BEWLEY WAY
GARDINERS CLO.
CRAVEN DRIVE
GOODMOOR CRES.
MARTINDALE RD.
ANDORRA WY.
BERRYFIELD GLADE
FARRANT AV.
PELHAM CRES.
ST. JOHNS AV.
STANSBY CR.
MOSELLE DRL.
GOLDEN VALE
QUINTON CL.
GOLDEN VALLEY BY-PASS
A40
Gloucester
Playing Field
Churchdown School
Parton Court
STATION ROAD
Churchdown
SUMMERLAND DR.
DOWDING WY.
TRUBSHAW CL.
HARRIS CL.
BADER CL.
SHACKLETON CL.
SWORDFISH CL.
BARNES WALLIS CT.
SUNDERLAND CT.
LYSANDER CT.
AVENUE
PARTON RD
PARTON CL.
PARTON DR.
COCHRAN CL.
COOK CT.
STATION CL.
PIRTON LANE
PIRTON MDW.
TALL ELMS CL.
WATERMOOR CT.
PIRTON CRES.
MELVILLE ROAD
St. Andrews Grn.
WINSTON ROAD
Pirton Court
BUSH HAY
CHOSEN DRIVE
Latymer Croft
JOHN DANIELS WAY
Playing Field
FAR SANDFIELD
ALBEMARLE ROAD
CAVENDISH AVE.
Tynings Ct.
Clinic
The Plocks
KAYBOURNE CR.
Sports Ground
Chosen Hill School
BROOKFIELD LA.
ANNE HATHAWAY DR.
Lower
Churchdown Village Jun & Inf. Schs.
Play. Fld.
CORDINGLEY
CORDINGLEY CL.
THE AVENUE
SANDFIELD RD.
KENT CLO
THE PIECE
The Manor
ORCHARD DR.
BLACKSMITH LA.
HOWCROFT
BARNHAY
CHURCH ROAD
STATION LANE
Rec. Grd.
Sweetbriar Houses
CHAPEL HAY CL.
OBROOKFIELD
ORCHARD
KINGSCOTE CL.
CROFT CL.
PAYNES PITCH
OLDBURY
DUNSTAN GLEN
OLDBURY ORCHARD
VICARAGE CL.
GREEN LA.
DREWS CL.
DREWS COURT LANE
GL3
TEWKE
THE GREEN
GREEN
CRIFTYCRAFT LANE
BARROW HILL LANE
CRANHAM LA.
Chosen Hayes Farm
Witcombe Bridge
Tinkers Hill
Barrow Hill
BROCKWORTH ROAD
M5
M5-MOTORWAY
Woodfield Farm
St. Bartholomew's Church
Quarry
Zoons Court
A B C D
88 89
22 21 20 19
1 2 3 4 5 6
11
22

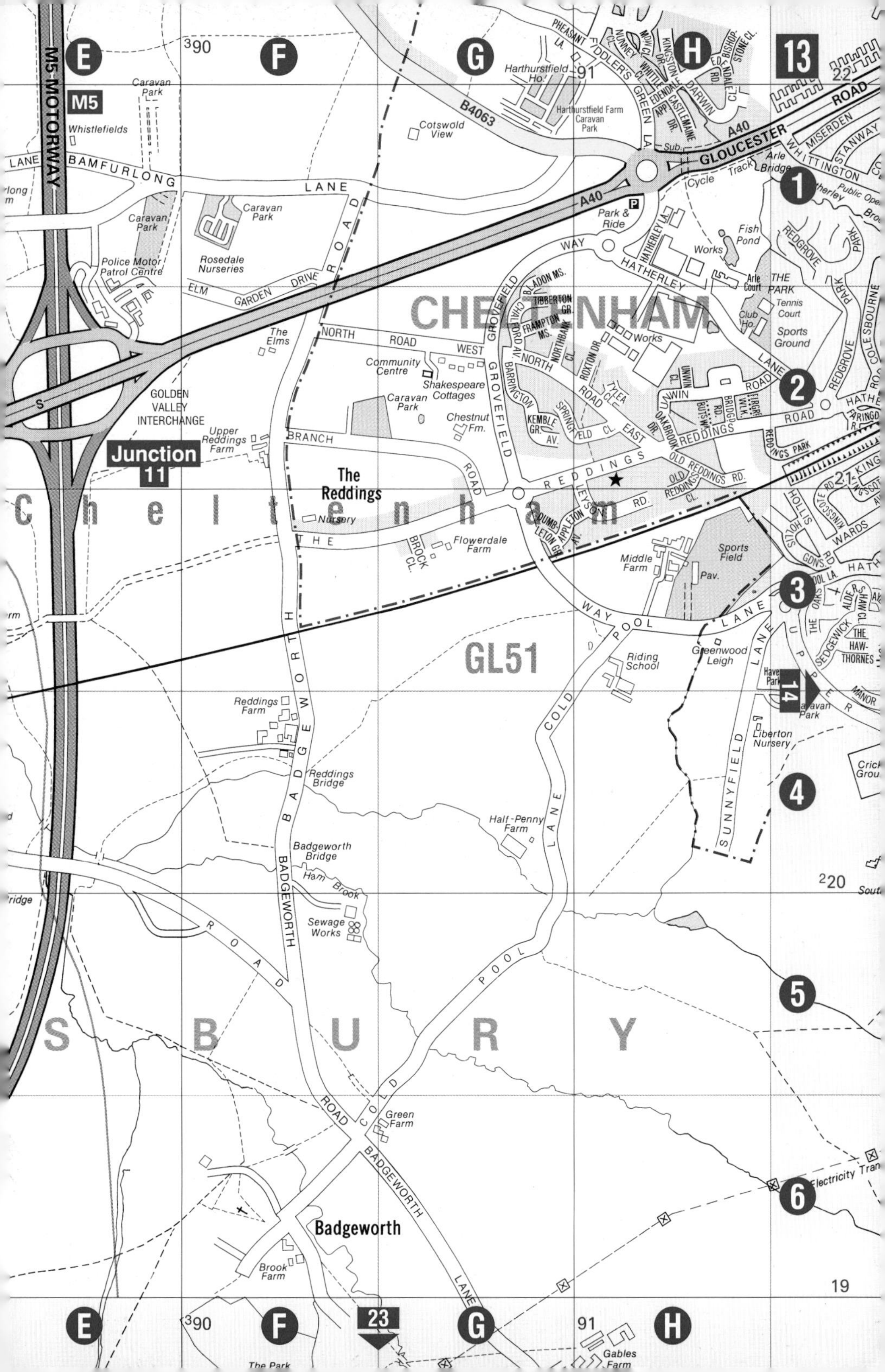

13
E
F
G
H
390
91
22
M5 MOTORWAY
M5
Caravan Park
Whistlefields
BAMFURLONG LANE
Caravan Park
Police Motor Patrol Centre
Rosedale Nurseries
ELM GARDEN DRIVE
Cotswold View
B4063
Harthurstfield Ho.
Harthurstfield Farm Caravan Park
PHEASANT LA.
FIDDLER'S GREEN LA.
A40
GLOUCESTER ROAD
Cycle Track
Arle Bridge
Park & Ride
HATHERLEY WAY
Fish Pond
Works
Arle Court
THE PARK
Tennis Court
Club Ho.
Sports Ground
CHELTENHAM
GROVEFIELD WAY
NORTH ROAD WEST
NORTH ROAD EAST
Community Centre
Shakespeare Cottages
Caravan Park
Chestnut Fm.
The Elms
GOLDEN VALLEY INTERCHANGE
Upper Reddings Farm
Junction 11
BRANCH ROAD
The Reddings
Nursery
THE REDDINGS
OLD REDDINGS RD.
BROCK CL.
Flowerdale Farm
Middle Farm
Sports Field
Pav.
Cheltenham
GL51
POOL WAY
POOL LANE
Riding School
Greenwood Leigh
14
Caravan Park
Liberton Nursery
Reddings Farm
BADGEWORTH ROAD
Reddings Bridge
Half-Penny Farm
COLD POOL LANE
SUNNYFIELD LANE
Badgeworth Bridge
Ham Brook
Sewage Works
220
SBURY
Green Farm
Badgeworth
Brook Farm
BADGEWORTH LANE
Electricity Tra
1
2
3
4
5
6
19
23
Gables Farm
The Park

Benhall
Hatherley
Warden Hill
Up Hatherley
GL51
CHELTENHAM SPA
TEWKESBURY
Dean Close School
Dean Close Jun. Sch.
County Police H.Q. ('A' Divn.)
THE COTSWOLD NUFFIELD HOSPITAL
Westal Court
Brookfield School
Westlands School
Cheltenham Bournside Sch. & 6th Form Centre
Playing Fields
Playing Field
Recreation Ground
Lakeside Prim. Sch.
Benhall Inf. Sch.
St. Mark's C.of E. Jun. Sch.
Public Open Space
Spoil Bank
Cloddymore Crossing
Hatherley Brook
Arle Bridge
Arle Court
THE PARK
Tennis Court
Sports Ground
Sports Field
Fish Pond
Works
Club Ho.
Pav.
Greenwood Leigh
Haven Park
Caravan Park
Liberton Nursery
Cricket Ground
South Park
Brick House
Greatfield
Comm. Cen. & Liby.
Superstore
Community Centre
Prim. Sch.
The Oaklands
Brizen Farm
Hafod
Oak Farm
Business Centre
Harford
Electricity Transmission Line
Shurdington Bridge
Church Farm
A40
A46
B4633
GLOUCESTER ROAD
LANSDOWN ROAD
HATHERLEY LANE
HATHERLEY ROAD
HATHERLEY RD.
UP HATHERLEY WAY
SHURDINGTON ROAD
MAIN ROAD
CHARGROVE LANE
WARDEN HILL ROAD
ALMA ROAD
CAERNARVON ROAD
GREATFIELD LANE
ROBERT NETTLETON ROAD
BIBURY ROAD
CAMPDEN ROAD
SALISBURY AVENUE
CANTERBURY WALK
WINCHESTER WAY
SUNNYFIELD LANE
UPPER HATHERLEY
COLD POOL LA.
LECKHAMPTON
A B C D
1 2 3 4 5 6
92 93
19 20 21 22
4 13 24

E
F
G
H
5
15
16
25
94
395
1
2
3
4
5
6
20
21
22
Bayshill
Lansdown
Montpellier
Montpellier Gdns.
Tivoli
The Park
Playing Field
GL50
GL53
Cheltenham College
College Sports Grd.
CHELTENHAM GENERAL HOSPITAL
Sandford Pool
Sandford Mill (Disused)
Public Open Space
Thirlestaine Court
Charlton Park
E. Gloucestershire Lawn Tennis & Hockey Club's Grd.
Cheltenham Croquet Club's Grd.
Naunton Primary School
Naunton Park
Swimming Pool
CHARLTON KINGS
Delancey Hospital (Mental Health)
Delancey Hosp. (Geriatric)
Pilley
Sandy La. Play. Fld.
Richard Pate Junior School
Southfield Manor
Burrow's Sports Ground
Leckhampton C. of E. Prim. Sch.
Leckhampton
Sue Ryder Home for Palliative Care
Leckhampton Court
Reservoir
Kennels
Church Farm
Elm Farm
Broadwell
Red Bungalow
Rectory
Moat
The Vineries
Brizon Cottage
Leckhampton Industrial Estate
Warehouse
Nursery
Cheltenham College Jun. Sch.
Cotswold Play. Fld.
The Lake
The Park Campus
Sports Hall
LANSDOWN ROAD
A40
A46
BATH ROAD
SANDFORD ROAD
THIRLESTAINE RD.
LONDON ROAD
COLLEGE ROAD
SUFFOLK RD.
ANDOVER RD.
OLD BATH ROAD
CHARLTON LANE
LECKHAMPTON ROAD
NAUNTON LANE
MOOREND PARK RD.
PARK PL.
HALL ROAD
CHURCH LANE
COLLUM END RISE
PILLEY LANE
UNDERCLIFF AV.
DAISYBANK RD.
LECKHAMPTON HILL
KIDNAPPERS LANE

16
A
B
C
D
1
2
3
4
5
6
6
15
396
97
19
22
21
220
GL52
GL53
Battledown Hill
Sports Ground
Holy Apostles C.of E. Prim. Sch.
Hewlett's Camp
Battledown Manor
Battledown
Ben Venue
The Firs
Ashley Rise
Green Acres Fm.
Oakfield
Greenway Farm
Queen Elizabeth Playing Field
Coltham Fields
Ind. Est.
Tr. Est.
St. Edward's Junior Sch.
Castle Farm
Playing Fields
Cricket Gnd.
Tennis Courts
Playing Fields
Coronation Flats
Home Farm Cl.
Clinic
Sandford Pool
SANDFORD PK. TRAD. EST.
Fire & Rescue Services H.Q.
Coll. Baths
Sandford Mill (Disused)
River Chelt
Public Open Space
Thirlestaine Court
Sandringham Ct.
Charlton Park
E. Gloucestershire Lawn Tennis & Hockey Club's Grd.
Cheltenham Croquet Club's
Charlton Ho.
Hockey Pitch & Tennis Cts.
St. Edward's School
Playing Field
Church Hall
Cudnall
Spring Bottom
Spring Bridge
Swim. Pool
Ryeworth
Ham
Glenfield County Primary School
Springfield
Courtfield
East Court
East End
Balcarras House
Balcarras School
Balcarras Court
Jun. Sch.
East End Fm.
Charlton Kings Inf. Sch.
Coopers Ct.
Liby.
Tennis Cts.
Playing Field
Crab End
Cemetery
Beeches Play. Fld.
CHARLTON KINGS
Moor End
Moorend Park
Bafford House
Longleat Ho.
Little Pheasants
Gilbert Ward Ct.
Lilley Brook
Bafford Farm
Bafford
Bucklehaven
Up End
Little Herbert's
Nursery
Pilley
Sandy La. Play. Fld.
Southfield Brook
CHARLTON KINGS TRADING ESTATE
LILLEY BROOK GOLF COURSE
Lilley Brook
Southfield Manor
Southfield Farm Cottages
Lilley Brook Bridge
Reservoirs (covered)
Lilley Grove
Old Sand Pit
Timbercombe
Goss Covert
Jennings Grove
Ashgrove Fm
LONDON ROAD
CIRENCESTER ROAD
A40
A435
B4075
BATH RD.
OLD BATH ROAD
HALE'S RD.
KEYNSHAM ROAD
SANDFORD MILL RD.
BATTLEDOWN APPROACH
STANLEY ROAD
BIRCHLEY RD.
ASHLEY ROAD
GREENWAY LA.
RYEWORTH RD.
HAM ROAD
CUDNALL ST.
CHURCH STREET
EAST END ROAD
LYEFIELD RD. W.
LYEFIELD RD. E.
HORSEFAIR ST.
SCHOOL RD.
COPT ELM RD.
BROOKWAY RD.
MOOREND RD.
NEWCOURT RD.
CHARLTON PARK GATE
GREENHILLS RD.
SANDY LANE
SANDY LANE RD.
BAFFORD LA.
BAFFORD APPROACH
LONGWAY AV.
BEECHES RD.
SAPPERCOMBE LA.
LITTLE HERBERT'S RD.
TIMBERCOMBE LA.
HIGHLAND RD.
HARTLEY CLO.
LITTLEDOWN RD.
PARKLAND RD.
GADSHILL RD.
BALCARRAS RD.
HARTLEBURY WAY
CASTLEFIELDS AV.
LEDMORE RD.
BRADLEY RD.
GARDEN RD.
CROFT RD.
OKUS RD.
MORLANDS DR.
TIMBERCOMBE MS.
JAMES DROVE
RAVENSGATE RD.
WISTLEY RD.
CHATCOMBE CL.
WILLOW RD.
CHERRY AV.
BIRCH CL.
ASH CL.
CEDAR CL.
MAPLE DR.

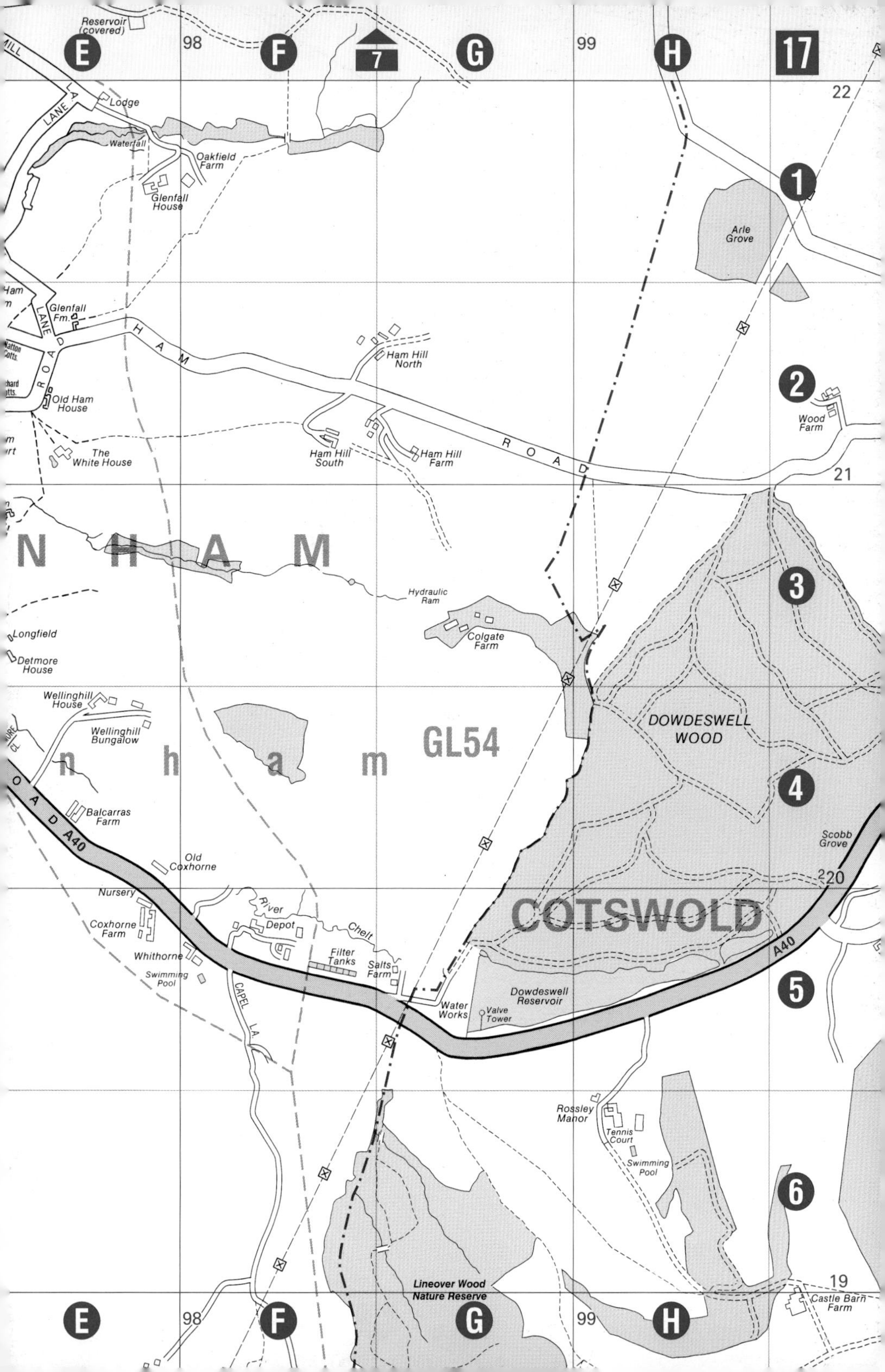

Reservoir (covered)
E
98
F
7
G
99
H
22
Lodge
Waterfall
Oakfield Farm
Glenfall House
Arle Grove
1
Glenfall Fm.
HAM ROAD
Ham Hill North
2
Wood Farm
Old Ham House
The White House
Ham Hill South
Ham Hill Farm
21
N H A M
3
Hydraulic Ram
Colgate Farm
Longfield
Detmore House
Wellinghill House
Wellinghill Bungalow
DOWDESWELL WOOD
GL54
n h a m
4
Balcarras Farm
A40
Scobb Grove
Old Coxhorne
220
Nursery
River Chelt
COTSWOLD
Coxhorne Farm
Depot
Whithorne
Filter Tanks
Salts Farm
Swimming Pool
CAPEL LA.
Dowdeswell Reservoir
5
Water Works
Valve Tower
Rossley Manor
Tennis Court
Swimming Pool
6
Lineover Wood Nature Reserve
19
Castle Barn Farm
E
98
F
G
99
H

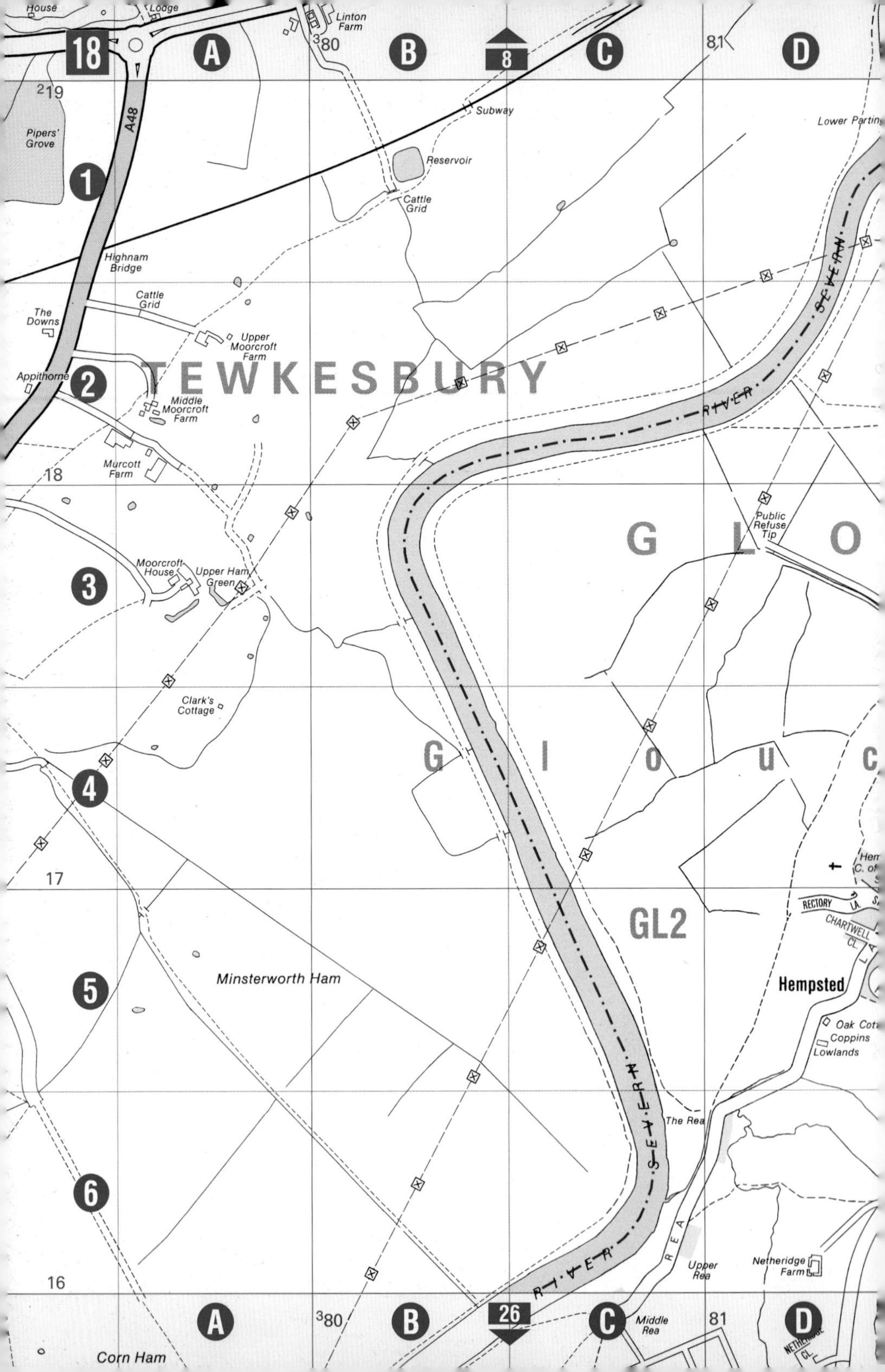

House
Lodge
Linton Farm
18
A
380
B
8
C
81
D
219
A48
Pipers' Grove
Subway
Lower Parting
Reservoir
Cattle Grid
1
Highnam Bridge
Cattle Grid
The Downs
Upper Moorcroft Farm
TEWKESBURY
Appithorne
2
Middle Moorcroft Farm
RIVER
SEVERN
Murcott Farm
18
Public Refuse Tip
G L O
Moorcroft House
Upper Ham Green
3
Clark's Cottage
G I O U C
4
17
GL2
RECTORY LA.
CHARTWELL CL.
Minsterworth Ham
5
Hempsted
Oak Cott
Coppins
Lowlands
The Rea
6
REA
RIVER SEVERN
Upper Rea
Netheridge Farm
16
A
380
B
26
C
Middle Rea
81
D
NETHERIDGE CL.
Corn Ham

E
F
G
H
9
19
82
83
1
2
3
4
5
6
20
27
GLOUCESTER
WESTGATE LEISURE AREA
King's Sch. Cricket Ground
Playing Field
Westgate Bridge
THE WESTGATE GALLERIA (SHOP. CEN.)
Castle Meads Transforming Stn.
OXLEASE
CASTLE MEADS
Cathedral
King's Sch.
Priory
Play. Field
County Records Off.
LONDON RD.
GOUDA WY.
BLACK DOG WY.
A430
THE A4301 QUAY
WESTGATE
Folk Mus.
Shire Hall
College Mus.
H.M. Prison
Trans. Mus.
Barbican Ct.
Guildhall
EASTGATE SHOP. CEN.
Lib.
Bus Sta.
Land Registry
Lib. Mus. & Art Gall.
Technical Coll.
Coun. Offs.
Antiques Cen.
Barge Semington
Merchants Quay
Tall Ships
Soldiers (Mus.)
Victoria Dock Marina
Robert Opie Collection
Waterways Mus.
COMMERCIAL RD.
SOUTHGATE STREET
A4301
Llanthony Bridge
Weir
LLANTHONY ROAD
SEVERN ROAD
SEVERNSIDE TRADING ESTATE
HEMMINGSDALE RD.
Business Park
High Orchard
Llanthony Priory (remains of)
Gloucester City F.C.
SPINNAKER RD.
ABBEY LANE
Works
COTSWOLD EDGE BUSINESS CENTRE
Llanthony Wharf
Baker's Quay
Warehouse
Cinema
THE PEEL CENTRE
St. Paul's
ST. ANN WAY
TRIER WAY A430
Monk Meadow Dock
MADLEAZE
MADLEAZE TRADING ESTATE
Petroleum Depot
MONK MEADOW RD.
MONK MEADOW TRADING ESTATE
Newark House
SANDALWOOD DR.
Sports Ground
Playing Field
Manor Farm
HEMPSTED
(Hempsted By-Pass Under Construction Est. Comp. Feb. 2000)
Towing Path
Canal
Timber Yard
Sharpness
Gloucester and
Chemical Works
Hempsted Bri.
Depot
LANE
ASHVILLE RD.
ASHVILLE INDUSTRIAL ESTATE
BRISTOL A430
BRISTOL ROAD
A430
SPA ROAD
Cedar Ho.
The Spa Pav.
Spa Field
THE PARK
Min. Golf Course
Health Cen.
BRUNSWICK ROAD
PARK ROAD
PARKEND ROAD B4072
STROUD ROAD
CLIFTON RD.
MOORLANDS TRAD. EST.
Coll.
BARTON ST.
Superstore
Farm Mews
B4072
ROBINSON ROAD
CHURCHILL ROAD
Youth Cen.
GL1
LINDEN ROAD
Rec. Grd.
Rec. Ground The Lannett
Linden Prim. Sch.
TREDWORTH ROAD
Jun. Sch.
Health Cen.
STANLEY ROAD
TWEENBROOK AV.
Playing Field
Ten. Cts.
THE OVAL
Play. Field
Calton Jun. & Inf. Schs.
Ribston Hall School (For Girls)
Play. Fld.
Linden
Sports Ground
Pav.
Tennis Cts.
Bowling Grn.
Rugby Football Ground
CALTON ROAD
AVENUE
Duke of Beaufort Ct.
PODSMEAD RD.
Athletic Ground
Podsmead
Playing Field
MILTON AV.
FINLAY ROAD
16

A
B
C
D
1
2
3
4
5
6
10
19
28
GL2
GL1
Wotton
GLOUCESTERSHIRE ROYAL HOSPITAL
WOTTON LAWN HOSP.
Redcliffe College
GLOUCESTER
Kingsholm Prim. Sch.
County Records off.
Bus Depot
Bus Sta.
Guildhall
Lib. Mus. & Art Gall.
Land Registry
Superstore
Leis. Cen.
Widden Family Unit
Prim. Sch.
New Olympus Thtre.
THE PARK
Min. Golf Course
Health Cen.
St. Peter's R.C. Jun. & Inf. Schs.
Ambulance Service H.Q.
Helipad
Community Centre
Playing Field
Depot
Sorting Office
GLOUCESTER RETAIL PARK
Adult Training Centre
EASTBROOK ROAD TRADING ESTATE
EASTERN AVENUE TRAD. EST.
Driving Test Centre
Electricity Sub Sta.
Retail Park
CEMETERY
Coney Hill
Coney Hill Prim. Sch.
Comm. Cen.
Factory
Works
Youth & Comm. Cen.
Day Cen.
Hatherley Inf. Sch.
Tredworth
Finlay Prim. Sch.
Central Technology College
Rec. Grd.
Saintbridge Sports Centre
Sports Court
Saintbridge
Pond
Robinswood
Play. Field
Calton Jun. & Inf. Schs.
Laurel Farm
A38
A430
A4302
B4063
B4073
B4072
LONDON ROAD
BARNWOOD ROAD
METZ WAY
EASTERN AVE.
EASTERN AVENUE
FINLAY ROAD
STROUD ROAD
TRIER WAY
PAINSWICK ROAD
CONEY HILL ROAD
BIRCH AVENUE
WESTERN ROAD
HORTON ROAD
BARTON ST.
INDIA ROAD
STROUD ROAD
TREDWORTH ROAD
CHELTENHAM RD.
ESTCOURT RD.
MEREVALE
RIVERSLEY ROAD
ELMBRIDGE
ARMSCROFT CRESCENT
NORTHBROOK RD.
SOUTHBROOK RD.
OVERBROOK CL.
WELLS
YORK ROAD
DURHAM
HIGHFIELD PL.
ASHGROVE AV.
MALMESBURY
SKYLARK WY.
CURLEW
HAWTHORNE
STONECHAT AVENUE
HERON
NORBURY AV.
BADMINTON RD.
ROBINSWOOD
BANEBERRY
RESERVOIR
SAPPERTON
NORTHFIELD
BATHURST
HARTLAND
CEMETERY RD.
TEDDINGTON GDS.
COTTESWOLD ROAD
ASKWITH
PINEWAY
WREN CL.
ALPINE CL.
RIVER Twyver

TEWKESBURY
Barnwood
HUCCLECOTE
Hucclecote Green
Abbeydale
GL4
GL3
STROUD
A417 BY-PASS
BARNWOOD A417 BY-PASS
A40/A417 BARNWOOD LINK RD.
BROCKWORTH BY-PASS
M5 MOTORWAY
M5
Golf Course
Recreation Ground
Factory
Works
Superstore
Offices
Depot
Hotel
Zoons Court
The Noake
GLOUCESTER GREEN
Playing Fields
Tennis Courts
Bowling Grn.
BARNWOOD BUSINESS CENTRE
Barnwood Prim. Sch.
Barnwood Park
Barnwood Park Sch. for Girls
Playing Field
Hospice
Jordan's Brook Ho.
Manor Gds
Castle Cottages
Hillview Co. Prim. Sch.
Cherry Gdns.
Gloucestershire Information Technology Cen.
Silverdale Pde.
Lib.
Comm. Cen.
Hucclecote Mews
Glenville Pde.
The Cedars
Dinglewell Jun. & Inf. Sch.
King George V Playing Field
The Hucclecote Curriculum Centre
Old Green Farm
ORCHARD CARAVAN PARK
GLOUCESTER TRADING ESTATE
Holly House
Fieldview
Clinic
Abbeymead Primary School
Playing Field
Heron Prim. Sch.
GLEVUM SHOPPING CENTRE
Wheatridge Cl.
Upper Barnwood Mill (Dis.)
HUCCLECOTE ROAD
ABBEYMEAD AVENUE
UPTON LANE
BARNETT WAY
CREST WAY
CHOSEN DRIVE
HILLVIEW DRIVE
MAYFIELD DRIVE
ZOONS ROAD
LARKHAY ROAD
CONWAY ROAD
DINGLEWELL
KINGSCROFT ROAD
ASHWOOD WAY
TREVOR ROAD
LOBLEYS DRIVE
GREEN LANE
CHURCH ROAD
ROMAN ROAD
HONEYSUCKLE DRIVE
ELDFARE
BROOKFIELD ROAD
BROCKWORTH
11
22
29
E
F
G
H
86
87
1
2
3
4
5
6
19
18
17
16

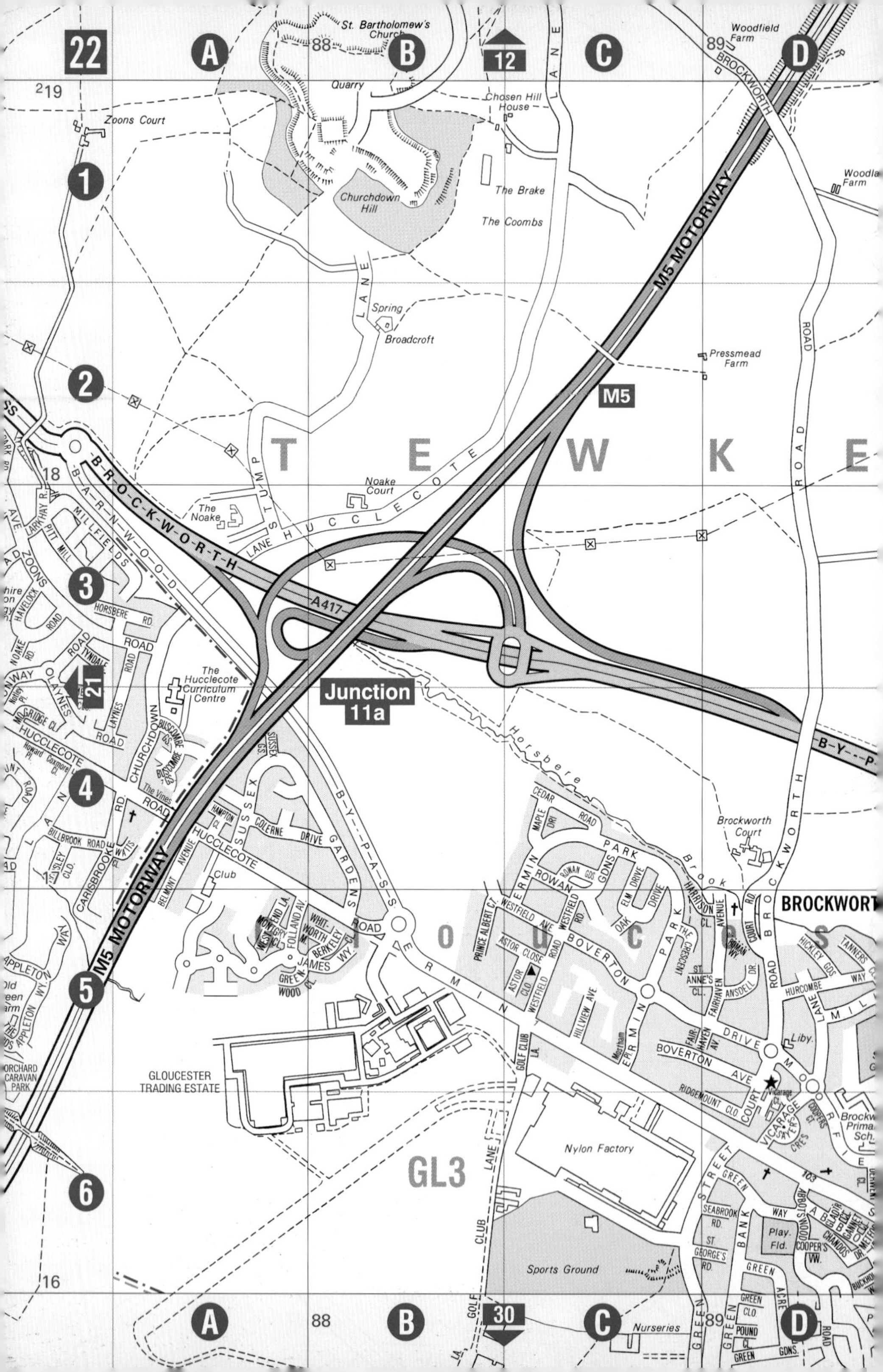
22
A
B
C
D
12
30
88
89
St. Bartholomew's Church
Quarry
Chosen Hill House
Woodfield Farm
BROCKWORTH
Zoons Court
Churchdown Hill
The Brake
The Coombs
Woodla Farm
M5 MOTORWAY
LANE
Spring
Broadcroft
Pressmead Farm
M5
ROAD
T E W K E
Noake Court
The Noake
HUCCLECOTE
STUMP
BROCKWORTH
BARNWOOD
MILLFIELDS
LARKHAY RD.
PITT MILL
ZOONS
A417
HORSBERE RD.
HAVELOCK ROAD
TYNDALE ROAD
OLAYNES
The Hucclecote Curriculum Centre
Junction 11a
Horsbere Brook
HUCCLECOTE ROAD
CHURCHDOWN
BUSCOMBE GDS.
The Vines
SUSSEX GS.
SUSSEX
COLERNE DRIVE
HAMPTON CL.
BYPASS
GARDENS
BILLBROOK ROAD
CARISBROOKE
WATTS
BELMONT AVENUE
Club
CEDAR ROAD
MAPLE DRI
ERMIN PARK
ROWAN GDNS
ELM DRIVE
Brockworth Court
HARRISON
AVENUE
COURT RD
BROCKWORTH
PRINCE ALBERT CT.
WESTFIELD AVE
WESTFIELD RD.
OAK DRIVE
BOVERTON
THE CRESCENT
ST. ANNE'S CL.
ROWAN WY.
ASTOR CLOSE
ASTOR CLO.
WESTFIELD ROAD
HILLVIEW AVE
ERMIN
FAIRHAVEN AV.
FAIRHAVEN
ANSDELL DR.
HICKLEY GDS
TANNERS WAY
HURCOMBE
LANE
MILL
Liby.
M5 MOTORWAY
APPLETON WAY
APPLETON WY.
ORCHARD CARAVAN PARK
MONTGRY CL.
WESTEND LA.
FOLLAND AV.
WHITWORTH M.
BERKELEY
JAMES WY. CL.
GREEN WOOD CL.
ROAD
GLOUCESTER TRADING ESTATE
GOLF CLUB LA.
BOVERTON AVE
DRIVE
RIDGEMOUNT CLO
COURT
VICARAGE
Brockw Prima Sch.
Nylon Factory
GL3
CLUB LANE
STREET
GREEN
SEABROOK RD.
ST. GEORGE'S RD.
BANK
WAY
Play. Fld.
COOPER'S VW.
CHANDOS
Sports Ground
GREEN
ACRE
GREEN CLO.
POUND CL.
GREEN GDNS.
Nurseries
GOLF LA.
219
18
16
1
2
3
4
5
6
21
103
BROCKWORT

Badgeworth
13
E
F
G
H
390
91
219
The Park
Brook Copse
BADGEWORTH
Gables Farm
Sunfield Farm
Badgeworth Nurseries
1
2
3
4
5
6
LAMBERT TERRACE
LAMBERT
LAMBERT DR.
School
GREENWAY CL.
LANE
ROAD
18
S B U R Y
Cheltenham
GL51
Dean Farm
Syringa Farm
Moat
Hunt Court
SANDY PLUCK
Brook Villa Farm
Bentham House
LANE
Norman's Brook
Works
24
Little Shurdington
Yew Tree Fa
A46
MAIN ROAD
A417
BROCKWORTH
Primrose Vale Poultry Farm
17
Windy Farm
DOG
The Elms
Playing Field
Play. Fld.
Mill Farm
Brockworth Sec. Sch.
Play. Fld.
LANE
GREEN LA.
Bentham Manor
Moat
Brockworth Hatchery
Orchard Farm
BENTHAM
LANE
ROAD
TAMAR
ROAD
TRENT
ROAD
HUMBER PL
RIBBLE CLO.
RIVERSMEET
CRESCENT
MEDWAY
HEB-DEN CL.
AVON
LEA
CLO.
ROAD
WYE
TONE DR
RD
ROAD
Henley
Ardencote Piggery
Bentham Indoor Sports Complex
SHURDINGTON A46
BY-PASS A417
Works
Middle Pig Farm
Poultry Houses
Bentham
Spring Orchard
16
Hall
Little Witcombe
31
Witcombe Court
Court Farm
Springfield Farm
MILL
BRYERLAND
PILLCROFT
LANE
Holly Brae
CIRENCESTER RD.
STREET
BENTHAM
LANE

A
B
C
D
92
93
14
23
219
18
17
16
1
2
3
4
5
6
Shurdington Bridge
Church Farm
School Lane
Blenheim Orchard
Playing Field
Church Road
Leckhampton View
Leckhampton Road
Sports Field
Lynfield Farm
Bickford House
Marsh Ter.
Cowls Mead
Woolsmead
Laurence Cl.
Vicarage Cl.
Lawn Cres.
Dutch Farm
Downfield House
Bishops Road
Roberts Rd
Home Farm
Lambert Terrace
Lambert Avenue
Atherton Cl.
Harrison Rd
Sinclair Rd
Poplar Farm
Shurdington
Badgeworth
Lambert Cl.
Wilson Rd
Gardens
Yarnolds
A46
Lambert Dr
The Orchard
Gr.
Shurdington House Stables
Farm La.
Shurdington Prim. Sch.
Greenway Cl.
Farm Lane
Nurseries
Shurdington Grove
Tewkesbury
Crippets
Cowley Farm
Main Road
Greenway
Orchard Farm
Hotel
Works
Shurdington Hill
Severn View
Reservoir (covered)
The Plantation
Little Shurdington
Greenway Farm
Cheltenham
GL51
Shurdington Court
Barrow Piece Plantation
Yew Tree Farm
Brook
Windy Farm
The Elms
Dog Lane
Greenfield Farm
Roman Villa (site of)
Dryhill Farm
Bekstone Farm
Bentham
Short Wood
Oakland Farm
Cold Slad
Crickley Hill
Works
Gloucester
GL3
Devil's Table
The Scrubbs
Bentham
Crickley Hill
Crickley Hill Country Park
Spring Orchard
A417
Brockworth By-Pass
Holly Brae
Crickley Court
Haroldstone House
Bentham Lane
A417

Kennels
E
94
F
15
G
395
H
219
DAISYBANK RD.
DAISYBANK ROAD
DAISYBANK
ROAD
Poultry House
CHELTENHAM
ROAD
Medley Green
Farm
Devil's Chimney
Settlement
Common Furze Wood
The Bittams
S B U R Y
Hill Farm
18
Leckhampton Hill
Engine House
Hartley Farm
LECKHAMPTON HILL
Blackhedge Farm
Salterley Grange
Pump House
n h a m
GL53
LANE
Hartley Wood
Ullenwood Court
17
Ullenwood
COTSWOLD HILLS GOLF COURSE
National Star Centre College of Further Education
Club House
Poolpiece Langet
Shortwood Flat
Shortwood Farm
Sports Ground
A436
A436
The Rise
Ullen Wood
Bookers
South Hill
Clerk's Patch
Town End
16
rove
GL4
1
2
3
4
5
6

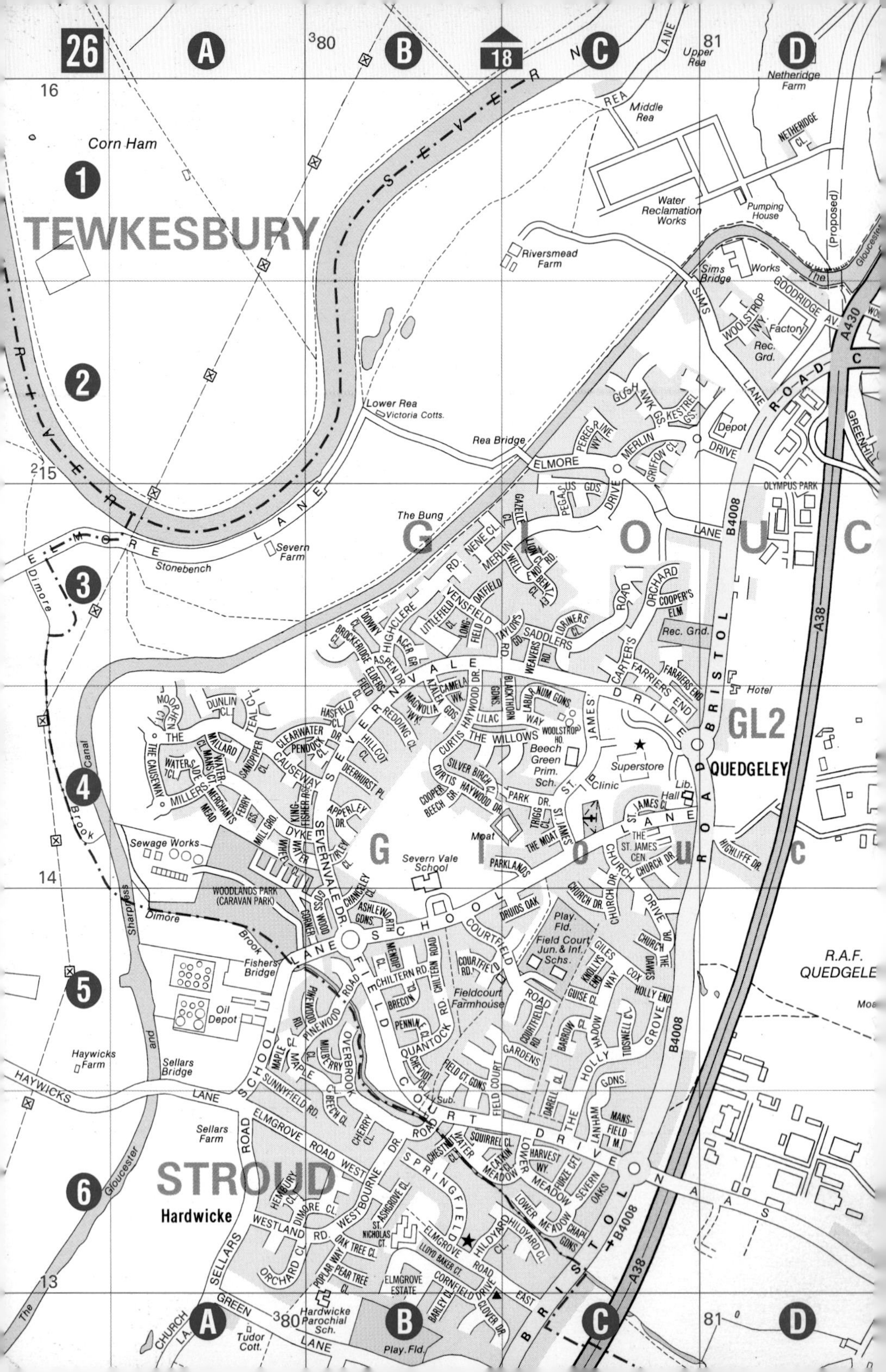
A
B
C
D
380
81
18
16
15
14
13
1
2
3
4
5
6
TEWKESBURY
STROUD
Hardwicke
QUEDGELEY
GL2
G L O U C
G I O U C
Corn Ham
R. SEVERN
Upper Rea
Middle Rea
Netheridge Farm
NETHERIDGE CL.
Water Reclamation Works
Pumping House
(Proposed)
Riversmead Farm
Sims Bridge
Works
Factory
Rec. Grd.
GOODRIDGE AV.
WOOLSTROP WY.
SIMS LANE
A430
Lower Rea
Victoria Cotts.
Rea Bridge
The Bung
ELMORE LANE
Severn Farm
Stonebench
Dimore
Canal
Brook
Sewage Works
WOODLANDS PARK (CARAVAN PARK)
Fishers Bridge
Oil Depot
Sharpness
Gloucester
Haywicks Farm
HAYWICKS LANE
Sellars Bridge
Sellars Farm
OLYMPUS PARK
Depot
Rec. Grd.
Hotel
Superstore
Clinic
Lib.
Hall
Beech Green Prim. Sch.
Moat
Severn Vale School
Play. Fld.
Field Court Jun. & Inf. Schs.
Fieldcourt Farmhouse
R.A.F. QUEDGELEY
ELMGROVE ESTATE
Hardwicke Parochial Sch.
Tudor Cott.
Play. Fld.
BRISTOL ROAD
B4008
A38
SEVERNVALE DRIVE
SCHOOL LANE
ST. JAMES
CHURCH DRIVE
FIELD COURT DRIVE
ELMGROVE ROAD WEST
ELMGROVE ROAD EAST
SELLARS ROAD
CHURCH LA.
GREEN LANE
NAAS LANE
MERLIN DRIVE
ELMORE LANE
THE CAUSEWAY
WESTLAND RD.
WESTBOURNE DR.
SPRINGFIELD
HOLLY GROVE

27
19
28
E
F
G
H
1
2
3
4
5
6
82
83
16
15
14
13
GL1
GL4
Podsmead
TUFFLEY
Lower Tuffley
Whaddon
ROBINS WOOD HILL COUNTRY PARK
STROUD
SOUTHERN AV.
A38
A430
A4173
B4072
STROUD ROAD
FINLAY RD.
TUFFLEY LANE
GRANGE ROAD
PODSMEAD RD.
Tuffley Trading Estate
Central Trading Estate
Capitol Park
Depot
Warehouse
Play. Field
Athletic Ground
Crypt Grammar School
Rugby Football Ground
Bowling Grn.
Duke of Beaufort Ct.
Grange Jun. Sch.
Grange Inf. Sch.
Rec. Grd.
Rec. Grd. Comm. Cen.
Homeleigh Park
Pitch & Putt Course
Library & Comm. Cen.
Beaufort Comm. Sch.
Harewood Jun. & Inf. Sch.
St. Peter's R.C. High Sch. & Sixth Form Cen.
Playing Field
Tuffley Prim. Sch.
Sewage Works
Manor Farm
Court Farm
Brook Farm
White House
Whaddon Green
Wynstones Rudolf Steiner Sch.
Whaddon Manor
Pound Fa
Robins Wood Hill Farm
Oakbank
Daniel's Brook
Sharpness Canal
Works
Play. Fld.
NEEDHAM AV.
GILBERTS LA.
CHURCH LANE

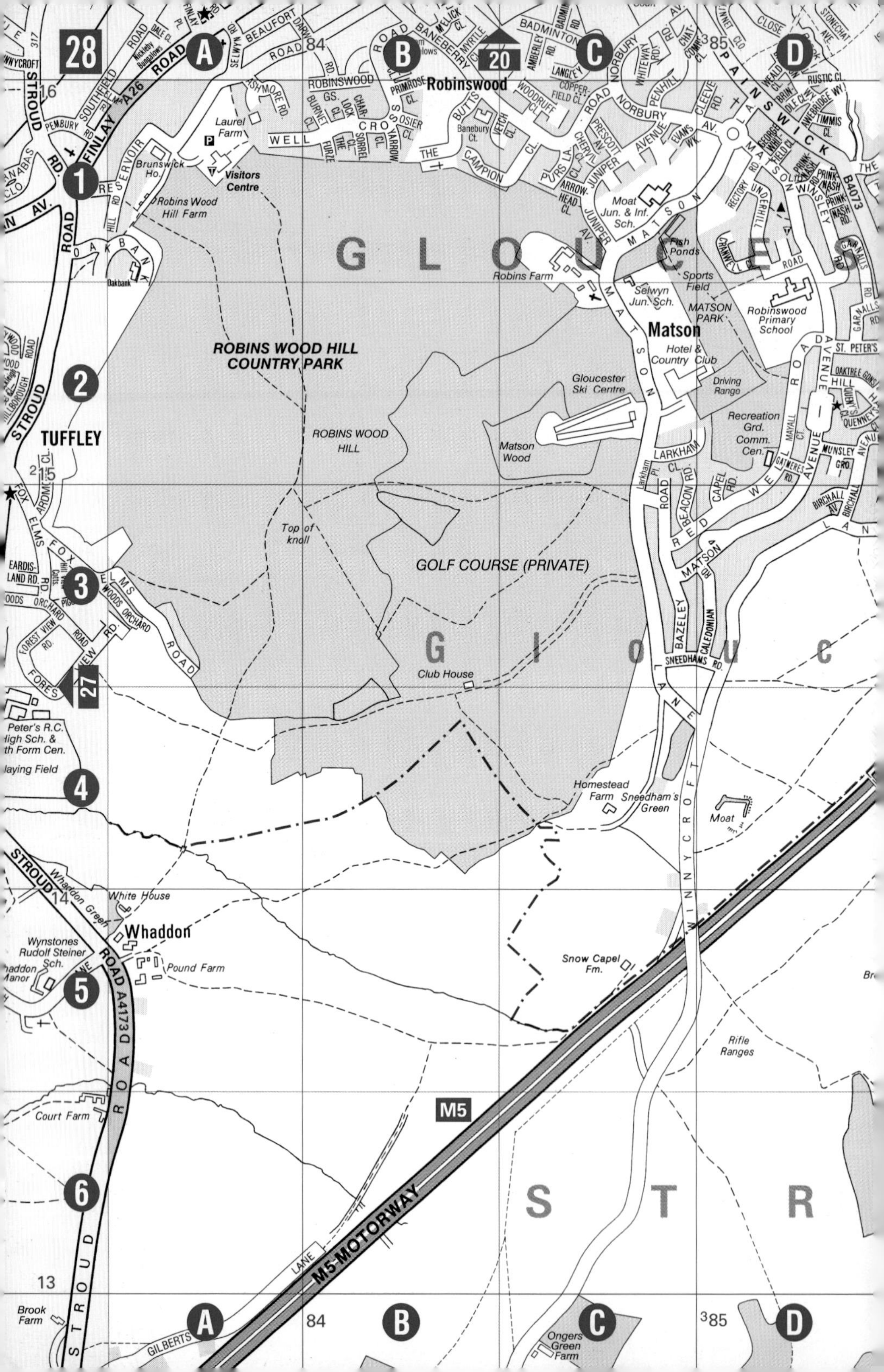

A
B
C
D
84
385
20
27
1
2
3
4
5
6
Robinswood
Laurel Farm
Visitors Centre
Brunswick Ho.
Robins Wood Hill Farm
Oakbank
G L O U C E S
ROBINS WOOD HILL COUNTRY PARK
ROBINS WOOD HILL
Top of knoll
GOLF COURSE (PRIVATE)
Club House
Robins Farm
Moat Jun. & Inf. Sch.
Fish Ponds
Sports Field
Selwyn Jun. Sch.
MATSON PARK
Matson
Robinswood Primary School
Hotel & Country Club
Gloucester Ski Centre
Driving Range
Matson Wood
Recreation Grd.
Comm. Cen.
TUFFLEY
Homestead Farm
Sneedham's Green
Moat
White House
Whaddon
Wynstones Rudolf Steiner Sch.
Pound Farm
Snow Capel Fm.
Rifle Ranges
Court Farm
M5
M5-MOTORWAY
S T R
Brook Farm
Ongers Green Farm
STROUD ROAD
FINLAY ROAD A26
PAINSWICK ROAD B4073
MATSON LANE
WINNYCROFT LANE
MATSON AVENUE
JUNIPER AVENUE
NORBURY AVENUE
RESERVOIR ROAD
OAKBANK
WELL CROSS ROAD
THE CAMPION
LARKHAM CL.
BEACON RD.
CAPEL RD.
BAZELEY
CALEDONIAN
SNEEDHAMS RD.
RED WELL ROAD
MAYALL CT.
AVENUE
FOX ELMS ROAD
FOREST VIEW RD.
ORCHARD ROAD
WOODS ORCHARD RD.
EARDISLAND RD.
ARDMORE CL.
STROUD ROAD A4173
GILBERTS LANE
Peter's R.C. High Sch. & Form Cen.
Playing Field

E
F
G
H
21
30
86
87
16
15
14
13
1
2
3
4
5
6
M5
M5-MOTORWAY
Playing Field
GLEVUM SHOPPING CENTRE
Upper Barnwood Mill (Dis.)
ABBEYMEAD
AVENUE
THE WHEATRIDGE
WHEATRIDGE
GLEVUM WAY
UPTON LANE
Elm Court Farm
Wheatridge
MEERSTONE
OXMOOR
WOODLAND GREEN
WOODLAND GROVE
CHURCHFIELD ROAD
BONDEND ROAD
BONDEND
SIX ACRES
Commelines Mill Farm
Bondend
Farm
Upton St. Leonards C. of E. Sch.
Bowden Hall (Hotel)
Nut Hill
NUT HILL
TWYVER CL.
TWYVER BANK
ST. LEONARDS CL.
PINLOCKS
Recreation Ground
BIRCHALL LANE
OLDWAY
HIGH STREET
PERRY ORCHARD
THE STANLEY
Upton St. Leonards
B4073
Winnycroft Cottages
Winnycroft Farm
BARLEYCROFT CL.
ASHCROFT CL.
St. Leonard's Court
Ockold End
Grove Court
HILL
Hill Farm
GL4
STANLEY WALK
Poole's Farm
Moorend Equestrian Centre
PORTWAY
Manor Farm
VALLEY COTTS.
VALLEY LA.
Portway Farm
Bayliss Farm
Gastrell's Farm
Moorend
Moorend Farm
WATERY LANE
UPTON
Hotel Tara
Brimps House
B4073 STOCKLEY WAY
Kites Hill
Kimsbury House
e s t e r
O U D

A
88
B
22
Sports Ground
C
D
16
GOLF CLUB LANE
GOLF CLUB LA.
Nurseries
Works
Works
GREEN
GREEN CLO.
POUND CL.
GREEN GDNS.
ACRE
BANK
KENNEL LA.
WATERMEAD LANE
GREEN STREET
ABBOTSWOOD
Play Fld.
COOPER'S
CHANDOS DR.
METEOR
89
1
T E W K E
Abbotswood Farm
2
Green Street
Hall
215
Nut Hill
NUT HILL
PAINSWICK ROAD
3
G I O U C
Well Close Farm
Coopers Hill
Whitley Court
29
Upton Wood
Pincott Farm
4
Brockworth Wood
GL4
14
Bayliss Farm
Gastrell's Farm
COTSWOLD
High Brotheridge
Lakes
Prinknash Abbey
5
Pottery
A46
Brotheridge Farm
Settlement
S T R O U D
PORTWAY
Rough Park
Prinknash Park
Buckholt Wood
Nature Reserve
6
BUCKHOLT
Earthworks
Witches Tump
Kites Hill
Prinknash Bird Park
13
Woodside Farm
The Grove
Cranham Corner
A
88
B
C
89
D
Daniels Grove

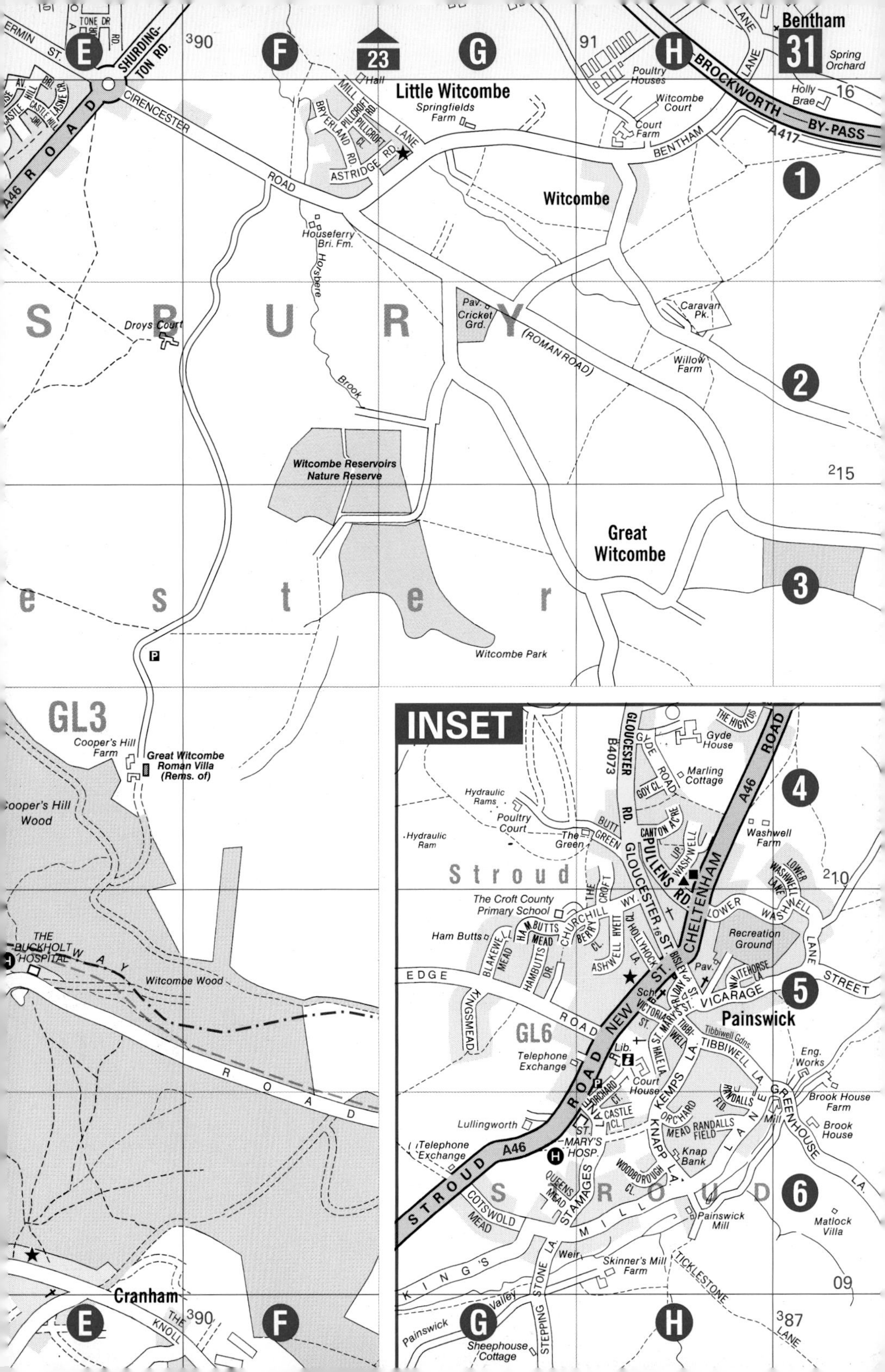

Bentham
Little Witcombe
Witcombe
Great Witcombe
Witcombe Reservoirs Nature Reserve
Witcombe Park
Great Witcombe Roman Villa (Rems. of)
Cooper's Hill Farm
Witcombe Wood
Cranham
INSET
Painswick
CIRENCESTER ROAD
BROCKWORTH BY-PASS
A417
A46 ROAD
STROUD ROAD A46
CHELTENHAM ROAD
GL3
GL6

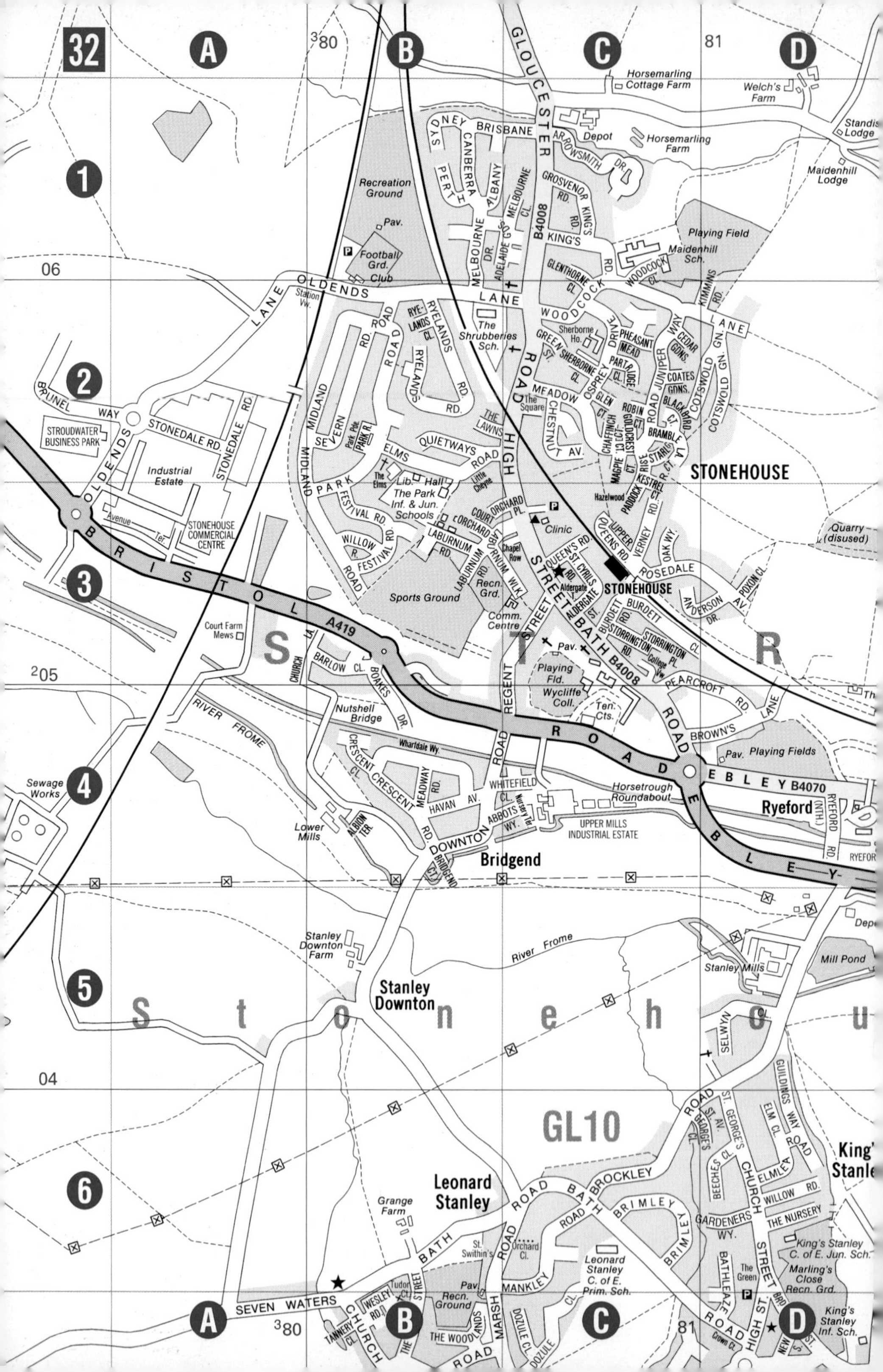

A
B
C
D
1
2
3
4
5
6
380
81
06
205
04
STONEHOUSE
Stonehouse
GL10
Bridgend
Ryeford
Stanley Downton
Leonard Stanley
King's Stanley
Recreation Ground
Football Grd.
Club
Playing Field
Maidenhill Sch.
Horsemarling Cottage Farm
Horsemarling Farm
Welch's Farm
Standish Lodge
Maidenhill Lodge
Depot
Industrial Estate
STROUDWATER BUSINESS PARK
STONEHOUSE COMMERCIAL CENTRE
The Shrubberies Sch.
Sports Ground
Recn. Grd.
Comm. Centre
Clinic
Lib. Hall
The Park Inf. & Jun. Schools
Wycliffe Coll.
Playing Fld.
Ten. Cts.
Quarry (disused)
Court Farm Mews
Nutshell Bridge
Sewage Works
Lower Mills
Horsetrough Roundabout
UPPER MILLS INDUSTRIAL ESTATE
Playing Fields
Stanley Downton Farm
Stanley Mills
Mill Pond
River Frome
Grange Farm
Recn. Ground
Leonard Stanley C. of E. Prim. Sch.
King's Stanley C. of E. Jun. Sch.
Marling's Close Recn. Grd.
King's Stanley Inf. Sch.
BRISTOL ROAD
A419
B4008
B4070
EBLEY
GLOUCESTER
OLDENDS LANE
HIGH STREET
BATH ROAD
REGENT STREET
SEVEN WATERS

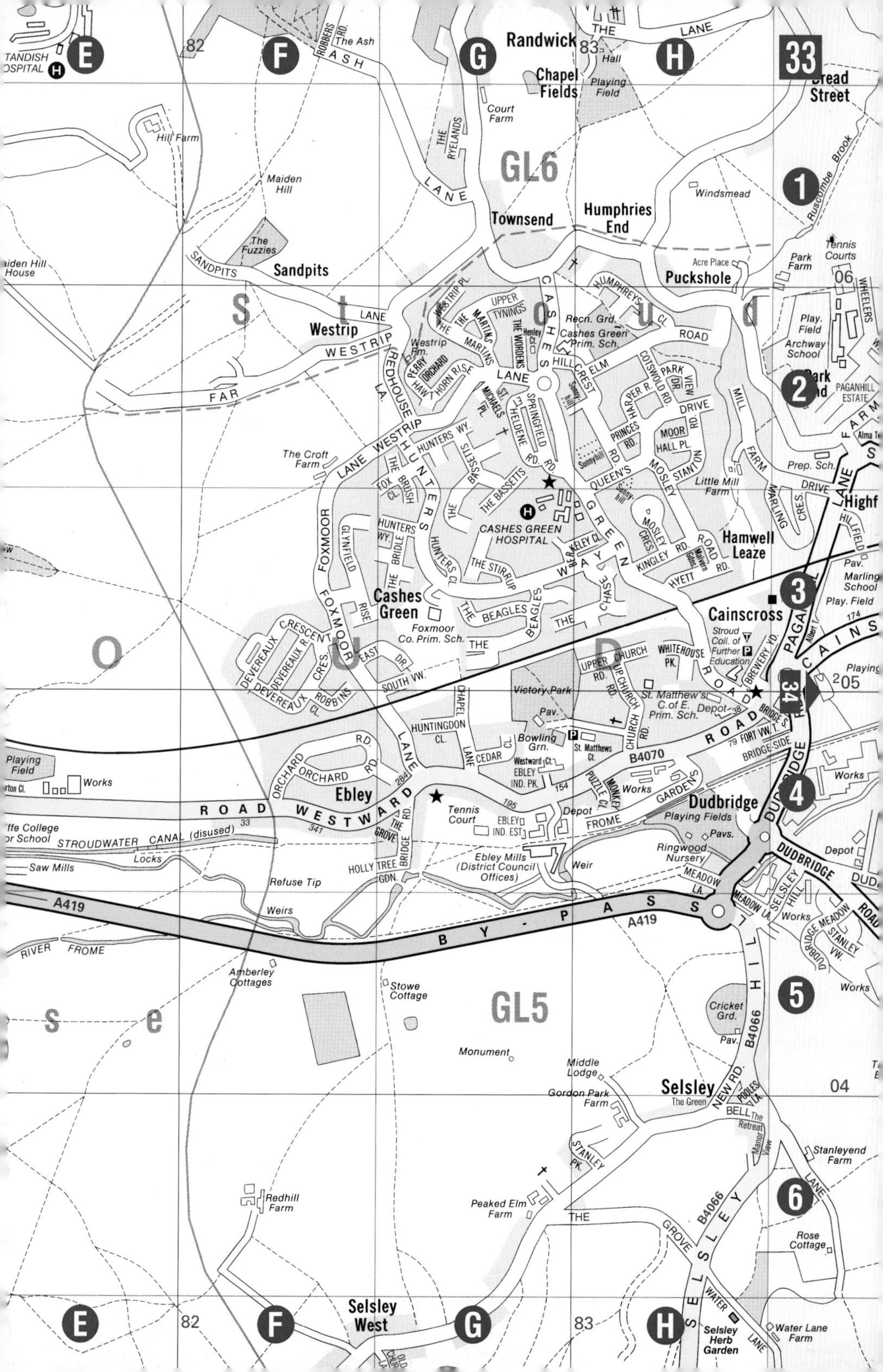
Randwick
Chapel Fields
Court Farm
Playing Field
Hall
Bread Street
Hill Farm
Maiden Hill
The Ryelands
GL6
Windsmead
Townsend
Humphries End
The Fuzzies
Sandpits
Puckshole
Acre Place
Park Farm
Tennis Courts
Westrip
Recn. Grd.
Cashes Green Prim. Sch.
Play. Field
Archway School
Paganhill Estate
The Croft Farm
Little Mill Farm
Prep. Sch.
Cashes Green Hospital
Hamwell Leaze
Marling School
Play. Field
Cashes Green
Foxmoor Co. Prim. Sch.
Cainscross
Stroud Coll. of Further Education
Victory Park
Pav.
Bowling Grn.
St. Matthew's C.of E. Prim. Sch.
Depot
Playing Field
Works
Ebley
Tennis Court
Ebley Ind. Est.
Ebley Ind. Pk.
Dudbridge
Playing Fields
Pavs.
Ringwood Nursery
Stroudwater Canal (disused)
Locks
Saw Mills
Refuse Tip
Weirs
Weir
Ebley Mills (District Council Offices)
A419
By-Pass
River Frome
Amberley Cottages
Stowe Cottage
GL5
Monument
Cricket Grd.
Middle Lodge
Gordon Park Farm
Selsley
The Green
The Retreat
Stanleyend Farm
Redhill Farm
Peaked Elm Farm
Rose Cottage
Selsley West
Selsley Herb Garden
Water Lane Farm
Standish Hospital
Maiden Hill House
Stroud
Westward Road
Selsley Hill
B4066
B4070
Dudbridge Road
Cainscross Road
34

A
B
C
D
1
2
3
4
5
6
Bread Street
The Plain
Callowell
Puckshole
Paganhill
Stroud College of Further Education
Park End
Highfield
Hamwell Leaze
Cainscross
Badbrook
Beeches Green
STROUD
GL6
GL5
Rodborough
The Butts
Selsley
Lightpill
Stanfields
Rodborough Fort
Rodborough Hill
RODBOROUGH COMMON (N.T.)
Dudbridge
STRATFORD PARK
Painswick Valley
SALMONS SPRINGS TRADING ESTATE
33

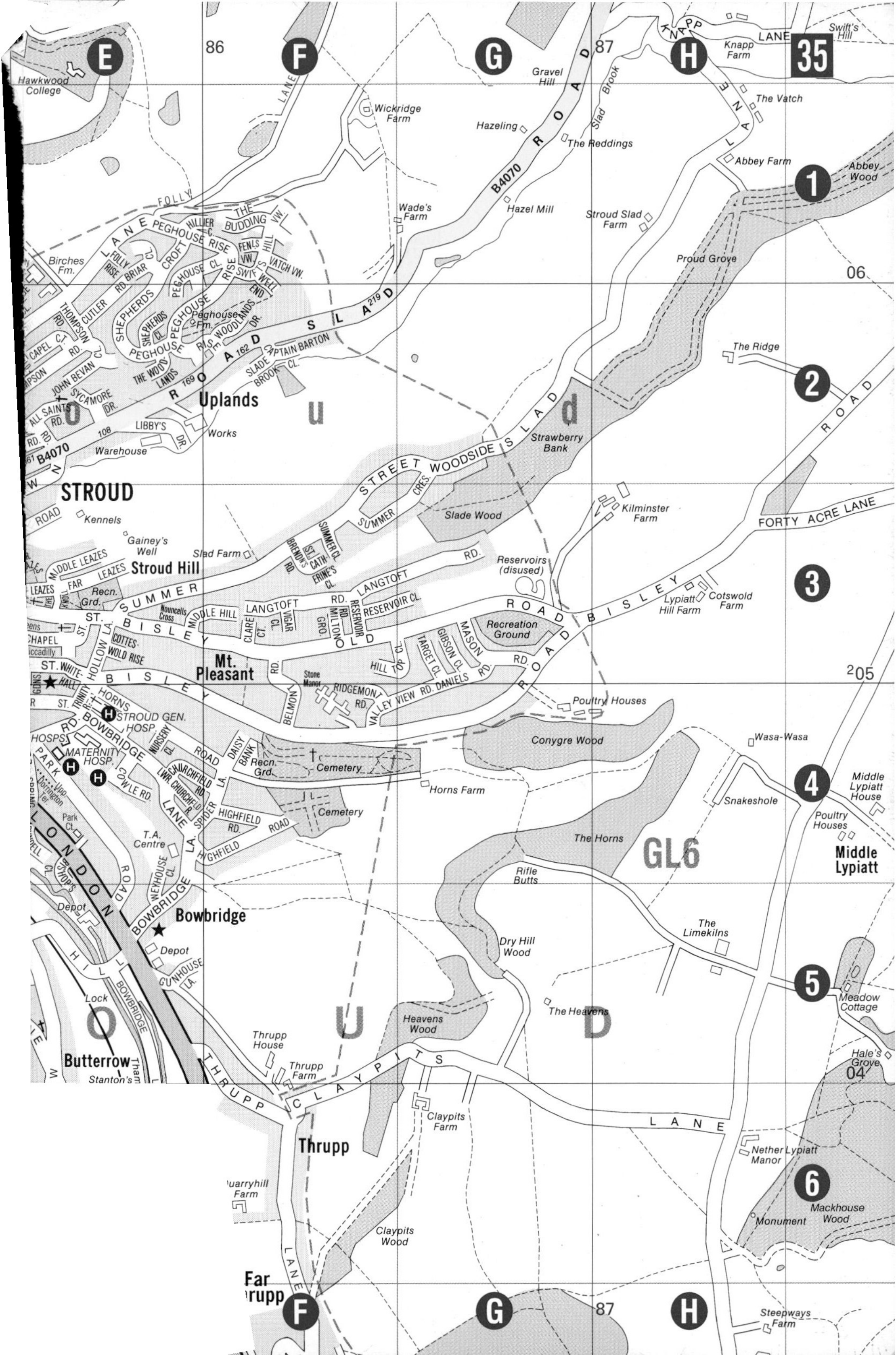
35
E
F
G
H
86
87
Hawkwood College
Wickridge Farm
Gravel Hill
Knapp Lane
Knapp Farm
Swift's Hill
The Vatch
Hazeling
The Reddings
Slad Brook
Abbey Farm
Abbey Wood
Wade's Farm
Hazel Mill
Stroud Slad Farm
Proud Grove
B4070 ROAD
SLAD ROAD
Birches Fm.
Peghouse Fm.
Uplands
Works
Warehouse
STROUD
The Ridge
Strawberry Bank
Slade Wood
Kilminster Farm
Forty Acre Lane
Kennels
Gainey's Well
Slad Farm
Stroud Hill
Reservoirs (disused)
Bisley Road
Lypiatt Hill Farm
Cotswold Farm
Recreation Ground
Mt. Pleasant
Stone Manor
Poultry Houses
Stroud Gen. Hosp.
Maternity Hosp.
Conygre Wood
Cemetery
Horns Farm
Wasa-Wasa
Snakeshole
Middle Lypiatt House
Poultry Houses
Middle Lypiatt
The Horns
GL6
Rifle Butts
T.A. Centre
Bowbridge
Depot
Dry Hill Wood
The Limekilns
Meadow Cottage
The Heavens
Heavens Wood
Lock
Butterrow
Thrupp House
Thrupp Farm
Claypits Lane
Hale's Grove
Claypits Farm
Thrupp
Nether Lypiatt Manor
Quarryhill Farm
Mackhouse Wood
Monument
Claypits Wood
Far Thrupp
Steepways Farm
1
2
3
4
5
6
06
05
04

INDEX TO PLACES & AREAS

with their map square reference

NOTES

1. Names in this Index shown in CAPITAL LETTERS followed by their Postcode District(s), are Postal Addresses.
2. The places & areas index reference indicates the approximate centre of the town or place and not where the name occurs on the map.

ABBEYDALE. (GL4) —6E **21**
Alstone. —5E **5**
Arle. —3C **4**

Badbrook. —2D **34**
BADGEWORTH. (GL51) —4F **13**
Bafford. —4B **16**
BARNWOOD. (GL3 & GL4) —2E **21**
BATTLEDOWN. (GL50 & GL52) —6B **6**
Bayshill. —6F **5**
Beeches Green. —3C **34**
Benhall. —1A **14**
BENTHAM. (GL3) —6H **23**
BISHOP'S CLEEVE. (GL52) —1F **3**
Bondend. —2G **29**
BOWBRIDGE. (GL5) —5E **35**
Bread Street. —1A **34**
BRIDGEND. (GL10) —4B **32**
Brockhampton. —4B **2**
BROCKWORTH. (GL3 & GL4) —5D **22**
Butterrow. —5E **35**
Butts, The. —5C **34**

CAINSCROSS. (GL5) —3H **33**
Callowell. —1B **34**
CASHES GREEN. (GL5) —2G **33**
Chapel Fields. —1G **33**
CHARLTON KINGS. (GL52 to GL54) —3H **15**
Charlton Park. —2A **16**
CHELTENHAM. (GL50 to GL54) —5F **5**
CHURCHDOWN. (GL3) —5C **12**
Coltham Fields. —1B **16**
Coney Hill. —4D **20**
Crab End. —4C **16**
CRANHAM. (GL4) —6E **31**
Cranham Corner. —6B **30**
Crickley Hill. —6D **24**
Crippets. —2D **24**
Cudnall. —3B **16**

DUDBRIDGE. (GL5) —4A **34**

East End. —4D **16**

EBLEY. (GL5) —4G **33**
Elmbridge. —1D **20**

Fairview. —6H **5**
Far Thrupp. —6F **35**
Fiddler's Green. —5A **4**

GLOUCESTER. (GL1 to GL4 & GL19) —4A **20**
GREAT WITCOMBE. (GL3) —3H **31**
Green Street. —2D **30**

Ham. —2D **16**
Hamwell Leaze. —3H **33**
HARDWICKE. (GL2) —6B **26**
Hatherley. —2B **14**
HEMPSTED. (GL2) —5E **19**
Henley. —6F **23**
Highfield. —3A **34**
HIGHNAM. (GL2) —6A **8**
High Orchard. —3G **19**
HUCCLECOTE. (GL3) —3G **21**
Hucclecote Green. —5H **21**
Humphries End. —1H **33**

INNSWORTH. (GL2 & GL3) —3E **11**

Kingsholm. —6A **10**
KING'S STANLEY. (GL10) —6D **32**

Lansdown. —1E **15**
Lassington. —2A **8**
LECKHAMPTON. (GL51 & GL53) —5G **15**
LEONARD STANLEY. (GL10) —6B **32**
LIGHTPILL. (GL5) —6B **34**
Linden. —5G **19**
Little Herbert's. —4C **16**
LITTLE SHURDINGTON. (GL51) —4A **24**
LITTLE WITCOMBE. (GL3) —1G **31**
LONGFORD. (GL2) —3A **10**
LONGLEVENS. (GL2) —5E **11**

Lower Tuffley. —3F **27**
Lynworth. —4B **6**

Maidenhall. —4A **8**
MAISEMORE. (GL2) —2D **8**
Marle Hill. —3G **5**
MATSON. (GL4) —2C **28**
Maud's Elm. —3E **5**
MIDDLE LYPIATT. (GL6) —4H **35**
Montpellier. —1F **15**
Moor End. —4A **16** (Cheltenham)
Moor End. —5G **29** (Stroud)
Mount Pleasant. —3F **35**

Noverton. —3E **7**

OVER. (GL2) —5C **8**
Overton Park. —6F **5**

PAGANHILL. (GL5) —2A **34**
PAINSWICK. (GL6) —5H **31**
Park End. —2A **34**
Park, The. —2F **15**
Pilley. —5G **15**
Pitville. —4A **6**
Plain, The. —1B **34**
PODSMEAD. (GL2) —1G **27**
Pool Meadow. —6F **9**
PRESTBURY. (GL50 & GL52) —3D **6**
Puckshole. —1H **33**

QUEDGELEY. (GL1 & GL2) —4C **26**

RANDWICK. (GL6) —1G **33**
REDDINGS, THE. (GL51) —2H **13**
Robinswood. —6B **20**
RODBOROUGH. (GL5) —4B **34**
Rowanfield. —5D **4**
RYEFORD. (GL10) —4D **32**
Ryeworth. —2C **16**

Saintbridge. —6C **20**
ST MARK'S. (GL51) —6B **4**
St Paul's. —4G **5** (Cheltenham)
St Paul's. —3G **19** (Gloucester)
St Peter's. —3E **5**
Sandfields. —4D **4**
Sandpits. —1F **33**
SELSLEY. (GL5) —6H **33**
SELSLEY WEST. (GL5) —6F **33**
SHURDINGTON. (GL51) —1B **24**
SOUTHAM. (GL52) —5H **3**
Spring Bottom. —3C **16**
Stanfields. —6C **34**
STANLEY DOWNTON. (GL10) —5B **32**
STONEHOUSE. (GL10) —3C **32**
STROUD. (GL5 & GL6) —3D **34**
Stroud Hill. —3E **35**
SWINDON. (GL51) —1D **4**

THRUPP. (GL5) —5F **35**
Tivoli. —2F **15**
Townsend. —1G **33**
Tredworth. —5B **20**
TUFFLEY. (GL4) —3G **27**

UCKINGTON. (GL51) —1A **4**
ULLENWOOD. (GL53) —4E **25**
UP HATHERLEY. (GL51) —4B **14**
UPLANDS. (GL5) —2E **35**
UPTON ST LEONARDS. (GL4) —3G **29**

Vineyards, The. —5D **4**

WALHAM. (GL2) —4G **9**
Walham Green. —4G **9**
Warden Hill. —3C **14**
WESTRIP. (GL6) —2F **33**
Whaddon. —5B **6**
Wheatridge. —2E **29**
WITCOMBE. (GL3) —1H **31**
WOODMANCOTE. (GL52) —2H **3**
Wotton. —1B **20**

INDEX TO STREETS

HOW TO USE THIS INDEX

1. Each street name is followed by its Posttown or Postal Locality and then by its map reference; e.g. Abbeymead Av. *Abb* —4E **21** is in the Abbeymead Postal Locality and is to be found in square 4E on page **21**. The page number being shown in bold type.
   A strict alphabetical order is followed in which Av., Rd., St., etc. (though abbreviated) are read in full and as part of the street name; e.g. Aldershaw Clo. appears after Alders Grn. but before Alders, The.

2. Streets and a selection of Subsidiary names not shown on the Maps, appear in the index in *Italics* with the thoroughfare to which it is connected shown in brackets; e.g. *All Saint's Ct. Chel —5H **5** (off All Saint's Rd.)*

GENERAL ABBREVIATIONS

All : Alley
App : Approach
Arc : Arcade
Av : Avenue
Bk : Back
Boulevd : Boulevard
Bri : Bridge
B'way : Broadway
Bldgs : Buildings
Bus : Business
Cvn : Caravan
Cen : Centre
Chu : Church
Chyd : Churchyard
Circ : Circle
Cir : Circus
Clo : Close
Comn : Common
Cotts : Cottages
Ct : Court
Cres : Crescent
Dri : Drive
E : East
Embkmt : Embankment
Est : Estate
Gdns : Gardens
Ga : Gate
Gt : Great
Grn : Green
Gro : Grove
Ho : House
Ind : Industrial
Junct : Junction
La : Lane
Lit : Little
Lwr : Lower
Mnr : Manor
Mans : Mansions
Mkt : Market
M : Mews
Mt : Mount
N : North
Pal : Palace
Pde : Parade
Pk : Park
Pas : Passage
Pl : Place
Quad : Quadrant
Rd : Road
S : South
Sq : Square
Sta : Station
St : Street
Ter : Terrace
Trad : Trading
Up : Upper
Vs : Villas
Wlk : Walk
W : West
Yd : Yard

POSTTOWN AND POSTAL LOCALITY ABBREVIATIONS

A'dle : Abbeydale
Abb : Abbeymead
Badg : Badgeworth
Barn : Barnwood
Bat : Battledown
B'hm : Bentham
Bis C : Bishops Cleeve
Bow : Bowbridge
Brockw : Brockworth
Brook : Brookthorpe
Cain : Cainscross
C Grn : Cashes Green
Char K : Charlton Kings
Chel : Cheltenham
C'dwn : Churchdown
C Hill : Cleeve Hill
Cran : Cranham
Doc T : Docks, The
Dwn H : Down Hatherley
Dud : Dudbridge
Ebl : Ebley
Glos : Gloucester
Hard : Hardwicke
H'std : Hempsted
H'nam : Highnam
Huc : Hucclecote
Inn : Innsworth
K'ct : Kingscourt
King T : Kingsditch Trad. Est.
K Stan : Kings Stanley
L'dwn : Lansdown
L'hptn : Leckhampton
Leon S : Leonard Stanley
L'pll : Lightpill
Long : Longford
Longl : Longlevens
L Mills : Lower Mills
Mais : Maisemore
Mat : Matson
Nor : Norton
Olde : Oldends
Pag : Paganhill
Pain : Painswick
Pod : Podsmead
Pres : Prestbury
Qued : Quedgeley
Rand : Randwick
Red T : Reddings, The
Rod : Rodborough
Rye : Ryeford
Sandh : Sandhurst
Sel : Selsley
Sel E : Selsley East
Shur : Shurdington
Sthm : Southam
S'hse : Stonehouse
Stro : Stroud
Stro B : Stroudwater Bus. Pk.
Swin : Swindon
Swin V : Swindon Village
Thr : Thrupp
Tuf : Tuffley
Uck : Uckington
Ull : Ullenwood
Up Hat : Up Hatherley
Upl : Uplands
Upton L : Upton St. Leonards
Wtrp : Westrip
Whad : Whaddon
W'hll : Whiteshill
Wit : Witcombe
W'cte : Woodmancote

INDEX TO STREETS

Abbeyholme. *Chel* —6F **5**
Abbeymead Av. *Abb* —4E **21**
Abbey Rd. *H'std* —3F **19**
Abbots Clo. *Chel* —4E **15**
Abbots M. *Bis C* —3D **2**
Abbots Rd. *Abb* —5F **21**
Abbots Way. *S'hse* —4B **32**
Abbotswood Clo. *Tuf* —2G **27**
Abbotswood Rd. *Brockw* —6D **22**
Acacia Clo. *Pres* —2B **6**
Acacia Ct. *Chel* —5A **4**
Acacia Pk. *Bis C* —1C **2**
Acer Gro. *Qued* —3B **26**
Acomb Cres. *Char K* —3C **16**
Acre Pl. *Stro* —1H **33**
Acre St. *Stro* —3D **34**
Addis Rd. *Chel* —4E **5**
Adelaide Gdns. *S'hse* —1B **32**
Adelaide St. *Glos* —4B **20**
Admiral Clo. *Chel* —5A **4**
Aesops Orchard. *W'cte* —2H **3**
Aggs Hill. *Chel* —6E **7**
Albany. *S'hse* —1B **32**
Albany Rd. *Chel* —2E **15**
Albany St. *Glos* —4A **20**
(in two parts)
Albemarle Ga. *Chel* —3G **5**
Albemarle Rd. *C'dwn* —4C **12**
Albert Dri. *Chel* —3A **6**
Albert La. *Chel* —4G **5**
Albert Pl. *Chel* —5H **5**
Albert Rd. *Chel* —4A **6**
Albert St. *Chel* —4G **5**
Albert St. *Glos* —2A **20**
Albert Ter. *Stro* —3A **34**
Albion Pl. *Chel* —5H **5**
Albion St. *Chel* —5H **5**
(in two parts)
Albion St. *Glos* —2G **19**
Albion Ter. *L Mills* —4B **32**
Albion Wlk. *Chel* —5G **5**
Alder Clo. *Glos* —5D **10**
Alder Ct. *Chel* —5A **4**
Aldergate St. *S'hse* —3C **32**
Aldergate Ter. *S'hse* —3C **32**
Alders Grn. *Glos* —4C **10**
Aldershaw Clo. *Up Hat* —3A **14**
Alders, The. *Chel* —5E **15**
Alderton Clo. *Abb* —1F **29**
Alderton Rd. *Chel* —1B **14**
Aldridge Clo. *Chel* —4F **5**
Alexandra Rd. *Glos* —6B **10**
Alexandra St. *Chel* —2E **15**
Alexandria Wlk. *Chel* —5C **6**
Alfred St. *Glos* —3B **20**
Alington Clo. *Glos* —2B **20**
Allendale Clo. *Glos* —5D **10**
Allen Dri. *Stro* —2A **34**
Allenfield Rd. *Chel* —4F **15**
*All Saint's Ct. Chel —5H **5***
(off All Saint's Rd.)
All Saints' Rd. *Chel* —6A **6**
All Saints' Rd. *Glos* —3A **20**
All Saints Rd. *Stro* —2E **35**
All Saints' Ter. *Chel* —6A **6**
All Saints' Vs. Rd. *Chel* —6A **6**
Alma Clo. *Chel* —2C **14**
Alma Pl. *Glos* —4G **19**
Alma Rd. *Chel* —3C **14**
Alma Ter. *Glos* —4G **19**
Alma Ter. *Pag* —2A **34**
Almond Clo. *A'dle* —2E **29**
Almond Ct. *Chel* —5A **4**
Alney Ter. *Glos* —6F **9**
Alpine Clo. *A'dle* —5C **20**
Alstone Av. *Chel* —5E **5**
Alstone Croft. *Chel* —5E **5**
Alstone La. *Chel* —4C **4**
Althorp Clo. *Tuf* —3E **27**
Alverton Dri. *Bis C* —3D **2**
Alvin St. *Glos* —1H **19**
Amaranth Way. *Up Hat* —4C **14**
Amber Clo. *Tuf* —2F **27**
Amberley Rd. *Chel* —5B **4**
Amberley Rd. *Mat* —6C **20**
Ambrose Pl. *Chel* —5G **5**
Ambrose St. *Chel* —5G **5**
Anbrook Cres. *Huc* —4G **21**
Anderson Clo. *W'cte* —2G **3**
Anderson Dri. *S'hse* —3C **32**
Andorra Way. *C'dwn* —3A **12**
Andover Rd. *Chel* —1E **15**
Andover St. *Chel* —2F **15**
Andover Ter. *Chel* —1F **15**
Andover Wlk. *Chel* —2F **15**
Anlaby Ct. *Chel* —4H **5**
*Ann Edwards M. A'dle —1E **29***
(off Wayridge, The)
Anne Goodriche Clo. *Pres* —3D **6**
Anne Hathaway Dri. *C'dwn* —4D **12**
Ansdell Dri. *Brockw* —5D **22**
Ansell Clo. *Chel* —3C **14**
Apperley Dri. *Qued* —4B **26**
Apple Clo. *Pres* —2B **6**
Apple Orchard. *Pres* —2B **6**
Appleton Av. *Red T* —3G **13**
Appleton Way. *Huc* —5H **21**
Apple Tree Clo. *Abb* —1F **29**
Apple Tree Clo. *C'dwn* —2H **11**
Apple Tree Clo. *W'cte* —3H **3**
Aragon Way. *C'dwn* —2G **11**
Arcade, The. *Chel* —6H **5**
Archdeacon Ct. *Glos* —1G **19**
Archdeacon St. *Glos* —1G **19**
Archibald St. *Glos* —3A **20**
Archway Gdns. *Stro* —2B **34**
Arden Rd. *Chel* —4F **15**
Ardmore Clo. *Tuf* —3H **27**
Argyll Pl. *Glos* —1C **20**
Argyll Rd. *Chel* —1A **16**
Argyll Rd. *Glos* —1C **20**
Ariel Lodge Rd. *Chel* —5A **6**
Arkle Clo. *Chel* —2F **5**
Arle Av. *Chel* —5E **5**
Arle Clo. *Chel* —5E **5**
Arle Ct. *Chel* —1H **13**
Arle Dri. *Chel* —5D **4**
Arle Gdns. *Chel* —5D **4**
Arle Rd. *Chel* —4D **4**
Arlingham. *Up Hat* —4B **14**
Arlingham Rd. *Tuf & Saul* —1G **27**
Armada Clo. *C'dwn* —2G **11**
Armscroft Ct. *Glos* —2D **20**
Armscroft Cres. *Glos* —1C **20**
Armscroft Gdns. *Glos* —2C **20**
Armscroft Pl. *Glos* —2C **20**
Armscroft Rd. *Glos* —2D **20**
Armscroft Way. *Glos* —2C **20**
Arreton Av. *Glos* —5D **20**
Arrowhead Clo. *Glos* —1C **28**
Arthur St. *Glos* —2H **19**
Arundel Clo. *Tuf* —4F **27**
Arundel Dri. *Stro* —4C **34**
Arundell Mill La. *Stro* —4E **35**
Ascot Ct. *Glos* —3B **20**
Ash Clo. *Char K* —5C **16**
Ashcot M. *Up Hat* —4B **14**
Ashcroft Clo. *Mat* —3E **29**
Ashfield Clo. *Bis C* —2F **3**
Ashford Rd. *Chel* —2F **15**
Ash Gro. *Upton L* —2F **29**
Ashgrove Av. *Glos* —5D **20**
Ashgrove Clo. *Hard* —6B **26**
Ashgrove Way. *Glos* —4D **20**
Ashlands Clo. *Chel* —4B **4**
Ashlands Rd. *Chel* —4B **4**
Ash La. *Rand* —1F **33**
Ashlea Meadow. *Bis C* —1C **2**
Ashleigh La. *C Hill* —4H **3**
Ashleworth Gdns. *Qued* —5B **26**
Ashley Clo. *Char K* —2C **16**
Ashley Rd. *Char K* —2C **16**
Ashmead. *Glos* —4C **10**
Ashmore Rd. *Glos* —1A **28**
Ashover La. *Chel* —2F **15**
Ash Path, The. *A'dle* —1E **29**
(in three parts)
Ash Rd. *L'pll* —6B **34**
Ashton Clo. *A'dle* —2F **29**
Ashville Clo. *Glos* —6E **19**
Ashville Ind. Est. *Glos* —6F **19**
Ashville Rd. *Glos* —6F **19**
Ashville Trad. Est. *Chel* —2D **4**
Ashwell. *Pain* —5H **31**
Ashwood Way. *Huc* —5G **21**
Askwith Rd. *Glos* —5C **20**

Aspen Dri. *Qued* —3B **26**
Asquith Rd. *Chel* —3H **15**
Aston Gro. *Chel* —5A **4**
Astor Clo. *Brockw* —5C **22**
Astridge Rd. *Wit* —1F **31**
Asylum La. *Glos* —1B **20**
Athelney Way. *Chel* —1A **16**
Atherstone Clo. *Chel* —4A **4**
Atherton Clo. *Shur* —1A **24**
Attwood Clo. *Chel* —2B **4**
Augustine Way. *Abb* —5G **21**
Austin Dri. *Long* —3A **10**
Avebury Clo. *Tuf* —3E **27**
Avenall Pde. *Chel* —1A **16**
(in two parts)
Avening Rd. *Glos* —6A **20**
Avenue Ter. *S'hse* —3A **32**
Avenue, The. *Char K* —4H **15**
Avenue, The. *C'dwn* —4C **12**
Avenue, The. *Longl* —5E **11**
Avon Cres. *Brockw* —6E **23**
Avon Rd. *Chel* —5B **6**
Awdry Way. *Tuf* —3G **27**
Awebridge Way. *Glos* —1D **28**
Aycote Clo. *Glos* —6C **20**
Ayland Gdns. *Glos* —3B **20**
Aylton Clo. *Up Hat* —3A **14**
Aysgarth Av. *Up Hat* —4B **14**
Azalea Dri. *Up Hat* —4C **14**
Azalea Gdns. *Qued* —4B **26**

Bk. Albert Pl. *Chel* —5H **5**
Bk. Montpellier Ter. *Chel* —1F **15**
Bader Av. *C'dwn* —4B **12**
Badger Clo. *A'dle* —2E **29**
Badger Vale Ct. *Pod* —6F **19**
Badgeworth La. *Badg* —6G **13**
Badgeworth Rd. *Chel* —4F **13**
Badminton Clo. *L'hptn* —3G **15**
Badminton Rd. *Mat* —6C **20**
Bafford App. *Char K* —5A **16**
Bafford Gro. *Char K* —5A **16**
Bafford La. *Char K* —4B **16**
Bakehouse La. *Chel* —2E **15**
Baker St. *Chel* —4F **5**
Baker St. *Glos* —3G **19**
Bala Rd. *Chel* —3C **14**
Balcarras. *Char K* —4D **16**
Balcarras Gdns. *Char K* —4D **16**
Balcarras Retreat. *Char K* —4D **16**
Balcarras Rd. *Char K* —4D **16**
Balfour Rd. *Glos* —4G **19**
Ballinode Clo. *Chel* —2E **5**
Ballinska M. *Longl* —4E **11**
Bamfurlong La. *Chel* —1D **12**
Baneberry Rd. *Glos* —6B **20**
Banebury Ct. *Glos* —1B **28**
Bank, The. *Pres* —3D **6**
Barbican Rd. *Glos* —1G **19**
Barbican Way. *Glos* —1G **19**
Barbridge Rd. *Chel* —4B **4**
Barker's Leys. *Bis C* —1F **3**
Barley Clo. *Chel* —2A **4**
Barley Clo. *Hard* —6B **26**
Barleycroft Clo. *Mat* —3E **29**
Barlow Clo. *S'hse* —3B **32**
Barlow Rd. *Chel* —3C **4**
Barnaby Clo. *Glos* —4A **20**
Barnacre Dri. *Huc* —2G **21**
Barn Clo. *A'dle* —1F **29**
Barnes Wallis Way. *C'dwn* —4B **12**
Barnett Clo. *Chel* —2B **4**
Barnett Way. *Barn* —2E **21**
Barn Ground. *H'nam* —4A **8**
Barnhay. *C'dwn* —5B **12**
Barnwood Av. *Glos* —3E **21**
Barnwood Bus. Cen. *Barn* —2E **21**
Barnwood By-Pass. *Barn & Huc* —1E **21**
Barnwood Link Rd. *Glos* —5F **11**
Barnwood Rd. *Glos* —1C **20**
Barrack Sq. *Glos* —1G **19**
Barratts Mill La. *Chel* —6H **5**
Barrington Av. *Red T* —2G **13**
Barrington Dri. *Huc* —3G **21**
Barrow Clo. *Qued* —5C **26**
Barrowfield Rd. *Stro* —1B **34**
Barrow Hill. *C'dwn* —6C **12**
Barton Clo. *Char K* —5B **16**
Barton St. *Glos* —2A **20**
Barton Way. *Up Hat* —3B **14**
Barwick Rd. *Up Hat* —4C **14**
Base La. *Sandh* —1G **9**
Basil Clo. *A'dle* —1E **29**
Bassetts, The. *Stro* —3G **33**
Bateman Clo. *Tuf* —4G **27**
Bathleaze. *K Stan* —6D **32**
Bath Pde. *Chel* —1H **15**
Bath Rd. *Chel* —2G **15**
Bath Rd. *Leon S* —6B **32**
Bath Rd. *S'hse* —3C **32**
Bath Rd. *Stro* —5B **34**
Bath St. *Chel* —6H **5**
Bath St. *Stro* —3D **34**
Bath Ter. *Chel* —2G **15**
Bathurst Rd. *Glos* —5A **20**
Bathville M. *Chel* —1G **15**
Battledown App. *Chel* —1B **16**
Battledown Clo. *Chel* —6B **6**
Battledown Dri. *Chel* —1B **16**
Battledown Mead. *Bat* —6B **6**
Battledown Priors. *Chel* —6B **6**
Baynham Way. *Chel* —5G **5**
Bayshill La. *Chel* —6F **5**
Bayshill Rd. *Chel* —1F **15**
Bay Tree Clo. *Abb* —6G **21**
Bazeley Rd. *Mat* —3C **28**
Beacon Rd. *Mat* —3C **28**
Beagles, The. *C Grn* —3G **33**
Beale Rd. *Chel* —4A **4**
Beard's La. *Stro* —3B **34**
(in two parts)
Bearland. *Glos* —1G **19**
Beaufort Ho. *Glos* —3H **19**
Beaufort La. *Chel* —2A **16**
Beaufort Rd. *Char K* —2B **16**
Beaufort Rd. *Glos* —6A **20**
(in two parts)
Beaumont Dri. *Chel* —3A **4**
Beaumont Rd. *Chel* —3A **4**
Beaumont Rd. *Longl* —4D **10**
Beckford Rd. *Abb* —1F **29**
Beckside Ct. *Glos* —2A **20**
Bedford Av. *Chel* —5C **4**
Bedford Pl. *Stro* —3D **34**
Bedford St. *Glos* —2A **20**
Beech Clo. *Hard* —6B **26**
Beech Clo. *H'nam* —5A **8**
Beech Clo. *Pres* —3E **7**
Beechcroft Rd. *Longl* —4B **10**
Beeches Clo. *K Stan* —6D **32**
Beeches Grn. *Stro* —2C **34**
Beeches Rd. *Char K* —5C **16**
Beechurst Av. *Chel* —6A **6**
Beechurst Way. *Bis C* —1C **2**
Beechwood Clo. *Chel* —1C **16**
Beechwood Gro. *Tuf* —2H **27**
Beechwood Pl. *Chel* —6H **5**
Belfry Clo. *Barn* —3F **21**
Belgrave Rd. *Glos* —2H **19**
Belgrove Ter. *Glos* —4A **20**
Belland Dri. *Char K* —5B **16**
Belle Vue Clo. *Stro* —3D **34**
Belle Vue Rd. *Stro* —3D **34**
Bell La. *Glos* —2H **19**
Bell La. *Sel* —6H **33**
Bell Wlk. *Glos* —2H **19**
Belmont Av. *Huc* —5A **22**
Belmont Rd. *Chel* —5H **5**
Belmont Rd. *Stro* —4F **35**
Belmore Pl. *Chel* —1G **15**
Belworth Ct. *Chel* —2D **14**
Belworth Dri. *Chel* —2C **14**
Benhall Av. *Chel* —1A **14**
Benhall Gdns. *Chel* —6B **4**
Bennington St. *Chel* —5G **5**
Benson Clo. *Abb* —5F **21**
Bentham La. *B'hm & Wit* —6H **23**
Bentley Clo. *Qued* —3C **26**
Bentley La. *Sthm* —6H **3**
Berkeley Av. *Chel* —5H **5**
Berkeley Clo. *Huc* —5B **22**
Berkeley Clo. *Stro* —3G **33**
Berkeley Pl. *Chel* —6H **5**
Berkeley St. *Chel* —6H **5**
Berkeley St. *Glos* —1G **19**
Berry Clo. *Pain* —5H **31**
Berryfield Glade. *C'dwn* —3H **11**
Berry Lawn. *A'dle* —2E **29**
Berwick Rd. *Bis C* —1E **3**
Bethesda St. *Chel* —2G **15**
Betjeman Clo. *Glos* —1F **27**
Beverley Croft. *Chel* —5A **4**
Beverley Gdns. *W'cte* —2H **3**
Bewley Way. *C'dwn* —3H **11**
Bibury Rd. *Chel* —1B **14**
Bibury Rd. *Glos* —5A **20**
Bijou Ct. *Glos* —5A **10**
Bilberry Clo. *Abb* —1G **29**
Billbrook Rd. *Huc* —4H **21**
Billingham Clo. *Glos* —5C **20**
Billings Way. *Chel* —3E **15**
Birchall Av. *Mat* —3D **28**
Birchall La. *Upton L* —3E **29**
Birch Av. *Glos* —5C **20**
Birch Clo. *Char K* —5D **16**
Birches Clo. *Stro* —2D **34**
Birches Dri. *Stro* —2D **34**
Birchfield Rd. *Bis C* —1F **3**
Birchley Rd. *Bat* —1B **16**
Birchmore Rd. *Glos* —3B **20**
Birch Rd. *K'ct* —6B **34**
Birchwood Fields. *Tuf* —2G **27**
Birdwood Clo. *Abb* —1F **29**
Bishop Ct. *Chel* —5D **4**
Bishop Rd. *Shur* —1A **24**
Bishop's Cleeve By-Pass. *Bis C* —2D **2**
Bishops Clo. *Bis C* —2F **3**
Bishop's Clo. *Stro* —4E **35**
Bishops Dri. *Bis C* —2E **3**
Bishops Meadow. *Bis C* —1D **2**
Bishop's Rd. *Abb* —5F **21**
Bishopstone Clo. *Chel* —6A **4**
Bishopstone Rd. *Glos* —3B **20**
Bisley Old Rd. *Stro* —3E **35**
Bisley Rd. *Chel* —1B **14**
Bisley Rd. *Stro & E'cmbe* —3E **35**
Bisley Rd. *Tuf* —4H **27**
Bisley St. *Pain* —5H **31**
Bittern Av. *A'dle* —5D **20**
Blaby Clo. *Abb* —6G **21**
Blackberry Clo. *Abb* —1F **29**
Blackberry Field. *Pres* —4D **6**
Blackbird Av. *Inn* —3E **11**
Blackbird Ct. *S'hse* —2C **32**
Black Dog Way. *Glos* —1H **19**
Blackfriars. *Glos* —2G **19**
Blacksmith La. *C'dwn* —5C **12**
Blacksmiths Ground. *H'nam* —4A **8**
Blacksmiths La. *Mais* —2C **8**
Blacksmiths La. *Pres* —3C **6**
Blackthorn End. *Chel* —5D **14**
Blackthorn Gdns. *Qued* —3C **26**
Blackwater Way. *Inn* —4F **11**
Bladon M. *Red T* —2G **13**
Blaisdon Clo. *Abb* —1F **29**
Blaisdon Way. *Chel* —2B **4**
Blake Croft. *Chel* —3A **4**
Blakeney Clo. *Tuf* —2G **27**
Blakewell Mead. *Pain* —5G **31**
Bleasby Gdns. *Chel* —1D **14**
Blenheim Orchard. *Shur* —1B **24**
Blenheim Rd. *Glos* —3A **20**
Blenheim Sq. *Chel* —4B **4**
Blinkhorns Bri. La. *Glos* —2C **20**
Bloomfield Rd. *Glos* —4G **19**
Bloomfield Ter. *Glos* —5G **19**
Bloomsbury St. *Chel* —5F **5**
Bluebell Clo. *Abb* —6E **21**
Bluebell Gro. *Up Hat* —4D **14**
Boakes Dri. *S'hse* —3B **32**
Bodham Rd. *Chel* —3B **4**
Bodiam Av. *Tuf* —3E **27**
Boleyn Clo. *C'dwn* —2G **11**
Bondend Rd. *Upton L* —3F **29**
Bootenhay Rd. *Bis C* —1F **3**
Borage Clo. *Abb* —6G **21**
Boulton Rd. *Chel* —2G **5**
Bouncers La. *Pres* —4C **6**
Bournside Clo. *Chel* —2D **14**
Bournside Dri. *Chel* —2D **14**
Bournside Rd. *Chel* —2D **14**
Bourton Rd. *Tuf* —3H **27**
Boverton Av. *Brockw* —5C **22**
Boverton Dri. *Brockw* —5C **22**
Bowbridge La. *Pres* —2C **6**
Bowbridge La. *Stro* —5E **35**
Bowbridge Lock. *Stro* —5E **35**
Bowen Clo. *Chel* —4B **6**
Bowl Hill. *K'ct* —6B **34**
Bowly Rd. *Glos* —5G **19**
Bradford Rd. *Glos* —1C **20**
Bradley Clo. *Longl* —5D **10**
Bradley Rd. *Char K* —5B **16**
Bradshaw Clo. *Inn* —4F **11**
Brae Wlk. *A'dle* —1E **29**
Bramble La. *S'hse* —2C **32**
Bramble Lawn. *A'dle* —2E **29**
Bramble Rise. *Pres* —4D **6**
Bramley M. *Abb* —5H **21**
Bramley Rd. *Chel* —4C **4**
Branch Hill Rise. *Char K* —5B **16**
Branch Rd. *Red T* —2F **13**
Brandon Clo. *C'dwn* —1H **11**
Brandon Pl. *Chel* —3F **15**
Brecon Clo. *Qued* —5B **26**
Bredon Wlk. *Chel* —4C **6**
Bregawn Clo. *Bis C* —3D **2**
Breinton Way. *Longl* —4E **11**
Brevel Ter. *Char K* —4C **16**
Brewery Yd. *Stro* —3H **33**
Briarbank Rise. *Char K* —2D **16**
Briar Clo. *Stro* —1E **35**
Briar Lawn. *A'dle* —2E **29**
Briars Clo. *C'dwn* —3H **11**
Briar Wlk. *Pres* —4D **6**
Brickrow. *Stro* —3D **34**
Bridge Clo. *H'std* —5E **19**
Bridge Farm. *Mais* —2E **9**
Bridgend Ct. *S'hse* —4B **32**
Bridgend Rd. *Chel* —2H **13**
Bridge Rd. *Ebl* —4G **33**
Bridge-Side. *Cain* —4H **33**
Bridge St. *Cain* —4H **33**
Bridge St. *Chel* —3E **5**
Bridle, The. *Stro* —3G **33**
Brierley Clo. *Abb* —6F **21**
Brighton Rd. *Chel* —6A **6**
Brimley. *Leon S* —6C **32**
Brimsome Meadow. *H'nam* —4A **8**
Brindle Clo. *Glos* —1D **28**
Brionne Way. *Longl* —4C **10**
Brisbane. *S'hse* —1B **32**
Bristol Rd. *Glos* —5F **19**
Bristol Rd. *S'hse* —3A **32**
Britannia Way. *W'cte* —2G **3**
Brizen La. *Chel* —5D **14**
Broad Leys Rd. *Barn* —4E **21**
Broad Oak Way. *Chel* —3B **14**
Broadstone Clo. *Barn* —3F **21**
Broad St. *K Stan* —6D **32**
Broadway Clo. *Pres* —2B **6**
Broadwell Clo. *Abb* —6F **21**
Brock Clo. *Chel* —3G **13**
Brockeridge Clo. *Qued* —3B **26**
Brockhampton La. *Swin V* —6A **2**
Brockley Rd. *Leon S & K Stan* —6C **32**
Brockworth By-Pass. *Brockw* —2H **21**
Brockworth Rd. *C'dwn* —5D **22**
Brome Rd. *Abb* —6G **21**
Bronte Clo. *Chel* —2C **14**
Brook Ct. *Chel* —3E **15**
Brookfield La. *C'dwn* —4D **12**
Brookfield Rd. *C'dwn* —5C **12**
Brookfield Rd. *Huc* —4G **21**
Brooklands Pk. *Longl* —4D **10**
Brooklyn Clo. *Chel* —4C **4**
Brooklyn Ct. *Chel* —3D **4**
Brooklyn Gdns. *Chel* —4D **4**
Brooklyn Rd. *Chel* —5B **4**
Brook Rd. *Chel* —3D **4**
Brooksdale La. *Chel* —3F **15**
Brookside Clo. *Huc* —4G **21**
Brookside Vs. *Glos* —1C **20**
Brook St. *Glos* —3H **19**
(in two parts)
Brookthorpe Clo. *Tuf* —2G **27**
Brook Vale. *Char K* —2B **16**
Brookway Dri. *Char K* —3B **16**
Brookway Rd. *Char K* —3B **16**
Broom Bungalows. *Glos* —6B **20**
Brown Clo. *Chel* —4B **4**
Browning M. *Chel* —2C **14**
Brown's La. *S'hse* —4D **32**
Brunel Mall Shopping Cen., The. *Stro* —4D **34**
Brunel Way. *Stro B* —2A **32**
Brunswick Rd. *Glos* —2H **19**
Brunswick Sq. *Glos* —2H **19**
Brunswick St. *Chel* —5G **5**
Brush, The. *Stro* —2G **33**
Bruton Way. *Glos* —1A **20**
Bryaston Clo. *Chel* —5D **4**
Bryerland Rd. *Wit* —1F **31**
Brymore Av. *Pres* —2B **6**
Brymore Clo. *Pres* —2B **6**
Bryony Bank. *Chel* —5E **15**
Buckholt Rd. *Cran* —6B **30**
Buckholt Way. *Brockw* —6D **22**
Buckingham Av. *Chel* —5C **4**
Buckingham Dri. *C'dwn* —2H **11**
Buckland Clo. *Bis C* —2E **3**
Bucklehaven. *Char K* —4A **16**
Buckles Clo. *Char K* —4C **16**
Budding, The. *Stro* —1F **35**
Buddleia Clo. *Abb* —1G **29**
Buddleia Ct. *C'dwn* —2H **11**
Bullfinch Rd. *A'dle* —5D **20**
Bullfinch Way. *Inn* —2E **11**
Bullingham Ct. *Chel* —4F **5**
Bull La. *Glos* —1H **19**
Burdett Clo. *S'hse* —3C **32**
Burdett Rd. *S'hse* —3C **32**
Burford Dri. *Stro* —3B **34**
Burford M. *Glos* —3B **20**
Burgage, The. *Pres* —3C **6**
Burleigh Croft. *Huc* —3G **21**

Burma Av. *Chel* —5C **6**
Burnet Clo. *Glos* —1B **28**
Burns Av. *Glos* —1F **27**
Burton St. *Chel* —5F **5**
Buscombe Gdns. *Huc* —4A **22**
Bushcombe Clo. *W'cte* —1H **3**
Bushcombe La. *W'cte* —1H **3**
Bush Ct. *Pres* —4C **6**
Bush Hay. *C'dwn* —4A **12**
Bushy Way. *Chel* —2A **4**
Buttercross La. *Pres* —4E **7**
Buttercup Lawn. *A'dle* —2E **29**
Buttermere Clo. *Chel* —3B **14**
Buttermilk La. *C'dwn* —3B **12**
Butterow W. *Stro* —5C **34**
Butterrow Hill. *Stro* —5D **34**
Butterrow La. *Stro* —5E **35**
Butt Grn. *Pain* —4H **31**
Buttington. *Abb* —6G **21**
Butt's La. *W'cte* —1H **3**
Butts, The. *Glos* —1B **28**
Butts Wlk. *Chel* —2H **13**
Byard Rd. *Glos* —6E **19**
Bybrook Gdns. *Tuf* —4G **27**
Bybrook Rd. *Tuf* —4G **27**
Byfield Clo. *W'cte* —3H **3**
Byron Av. *Glos* —1F **27**
Byron Rd. *Chel* —6B **4**
Byron Rd. *Stro* —2A **34**

Caernarvon Clo. *Chel* —3B **14**
Caernarvon Ct. *Chel* —3A **14**
Caernarvon Rd. *Chel* —3A **14**
Caesar Rd. *Glos* —6F **19**
Cainscross Rd. *Stro* —3A **34**
Cakebridge Pl. *Chel* —4A **6**
Cakebridge Rd. *Chel* —3A **6**
Calderdale. *Abb* —6G **21**
Calderwood Ct. *Chel* —1G **15**
Caledonian Rd. *Mat* —3D **28**
Calspick Way. *Longl* —4E **11**
Calton Rd. *Glos* —6H **19**
Calverley M. *Up Hat* —4B **14**
Camberley Clo. *Huc* —4H **21**
Camberwell Rd. *Chel* —5A **4**
Cambray Ct. *Chel* —6G **5**
Cambray Pl. *Chel* —6H **5**
Cambridge Av. *Chel* —6C **4**
Cambridge St. *Glos* —2A **20**
Camellia Ct. *Up Hat* —4D **14**
Camellia Wlk. *Qued* —3B **26**
Camomile Clo. *Abb* —6G **21**
Campbell Clo. *Inn* —2F **11**
Campden Rd. *Chel* —1B **14**
Campden Rd. *Tuf* —2H **27**
Campion Clo. *Glos* —1B **28**
Campion Pk. *Up Hat* —5C **14**
Camp Rd. *Char K* —6C **6**
Cam Rd. *Chel* —4C **6**
Cams Ground. *H'nam* —4A **8**
Canada Ho. *Chel* —4B **4**
Canberra. *S'hse* —1B **32**
Canning Rd. *Inn* —5F **11**
Canterbury Wlk. *Chel* —3D **14**
Canton Acre. *Pain* —4H **31**
Cantors Ct. *Bis C* —3E **3**
Cantors Dri. *Bis C* —3D **2**
Capel Ct. *Pres* —3C **6**
Capel Ct. *Stro* —2E **35**
Capel La. *Char K* —5F **17**
Capel Rd. *Mat* —3D **28**
Capitol Pk. Ind. Est. *Glos* —1E **27**
Captain Barton Clo. *Stro* —2F **35**
Cares Clo. *Bis C* —1F **3**
Carisbrooke Dri. *Char K* —3D **16**
Carisbrook Rd. *Huc* —5H **21**
Carlton Gdns. *Stro* —3D **34**
Carlton Pl. *Chel* —4F **5**
Carlton St. *Chel* —6A **6**
Carlyle Gro. *Chel* —3A **4**
Carmarthen Rd. *Chel* —3A **14**
Carmarthen St. *Glos* —4A **20**
Carne Pl. *Glos* —2D **20**
Carrol Gro. *Chel* —3A **4**
Carter Rd. *Chel* —2C **4**
Carter's Orchard. *Qued* —3C **26**
Casey Clo. *Glos* —2C **20**
Cashes Grn. Rd. *Stro* —2G **33**
Casino Pl. *Chel* —2F **15**
Castle Clo. *Pain* —6H **31**
Castle Cotts. *Huc* —3G **21**
Castlefields Av. *Char K* —3D **16**
Castlefields Dri. *Char K* —3D **16**
Castlefields Rd. *Char K* —3D **16**
Castle Hill Dri. *Brockw* —1E **31**
Castlemaine Dri. *Chel* —1H **13**
Castlemead Rd. *Stro* —4C **34**
Castle Rise. *Stro* —4D **34**
Castle St. *Stro* —3D **34**
Castle, The. *Stro* —4D **34**
Castleton Rd. *Barn* —4E **21**
Catherine's Clo. *Stro* —3F **35**
Catherine St. *Glos* —6H **9**
Catkin Clo. *Qued* —6B **26**
Cattle Mkt. Ind. Est. *Glos* —5G **9**
Causeway, The. *Qued* —4A **26**
Cavendish Av. *C'dwn* —4C **12**
Cecil Rd. *Glos* —4F **19**
Cedar Clo. *Char K* —4C **16**
Cedar Clo. *Ebl* —4G **33**
Cedar Ct. Rd. *Chel* —1G **15**
Cedar Gdns. *S'hse* —2C **32**
Cedar Rd. *Brockw* —4C **22**
Cedars, The. *Huc* —3H **21**
Cedarwood Dri. *Tuf* —2H **27**
Celandine Bank. *W'cte* —1G **3**
Cemetery Rd. *Glos* —5B **20**
Central Cross Dri. *Chel* —4H **5**
Central Rd. *Glos* —4H **19**
Central Rd. *Stro* —3A **34**
Central Trad. Est. *Glos* —2E **27**
Central Way. *Chel* —5E **5**
Centurian Clo. *Abb* —5F **21**
Chaceley Clo. *Abb* —6F **21**
Chadbournes. *C'dwn* —3A **12**
Chad Rd. *Chel* —6C **4**
Chadwick Clo. *Tuf* —3G **27**
Chaffinch Clo. *Inn* —2E **11**
Chaffinch Ct. *S'hse* —2C **32**
Chalford Av. *Red T* —2G **13**
Chalford Rd. *Tuf* —4H **27**
Chamwells Av. *Longl* —5C **10**
Chamwells Wlk. *Longl* —5C **10**
Chancel Clo. *Glos* —3D **20**
Chanceley Clo. *Qued* —5B **26**
Chancel Way. *Chel* —3A **16**
Chandler Rd. *Bis C* —3E **3**
Chandos Dri. *Brockw* —6D **22**
Chandos Rd. *Stro* —6B **34**
Chantry Ga. *Bis C* —3D **2**
Chapel Gdns. *Qued* —6C **26**
Chapel Hay Clo. *C'dwn* —5B **12**
Chapel Hay La. *C'dwn* —5C **12**
Chapel La. *Chel* —2G **15**
Chapel La. *Ebl* —4G **33**
Chapel La. *W'cte* —2G **3**
Chapel Row. *S'hse* —3C **32**
Chapel St. *Chel* —5G **5**
Chapel St. *Stro* —3E **35**
Chapel Wlk. *Chel* —6G **5**
Chapman Way. *Chel* —2C **14**
Chargrove La. *Up Hat* —4A **14**
Charlecote Av. *Tuf* —5F **27**
Charlecote Corner. *Bis C* —2D **2**
Charles St. *Chel* —4F **5**
Charles St. *Glos* —2A **20**
Charlock Clo. *Glos* —1B **28**
Charlton Clo. *Char K* —4B **16**
Charlton Ct. *Glos* —1A **20**
Charlton Ct. Rd. *Char K* —2B **16**
Charlton Dri. *Char K* —2A **16**
Charlton Kings Trad. Est. *Char K* —5B **16**
Charlton La. *Chel* —4G **15**
Charlton Lawn. *Char K* —3B **16**
Charlton Pk. Dri. *Chel* —2H **15**
Charlton Pk. Ga. *Chel* —3H **15**
Charlton Way. *Longl* —4D **10**
Charnwood Clo. *Chel* —4G **15**
Charnwood Rd. *Chel* —4G **15**
Charter Ct. *Glos* —3A **20**
Chartwell Clo. *H'std* —5D **18**
Chase Av. *Char K* —3D **16**
Chasely Cres. *Up Hat* —4B **14**
Chase, The. *A'dle* —6E **21**
Chase, The. *Stro* —3H **33**
Chatcombe Clo. *Char K* —5C **16**
Chatcombe Rd. *Mat* —6C **20**
Chatsworth Av. *Tuf* —4F **27**
Chatsworth Dri. *Chel* —5G **15**
Chaucer Clo. *Glos* —6G **19**
Cheapside. *Stro* —3C **34**
Chedworth Rd. *Tuf* —2H **27**
Chedworth Way. *Chel* —1B **14**
Chelmsford Av. *Chel* —4D **14**
Chelsea Clo. *Chel* —2A **16**
Cheltenham Rd. *Bis C* —5E **3**
Cheltenham Rd. *Glos* —6C **10**
Cheltenham Rd. *Pain* —5H **31**
Cheltenham Rd. E. *Glos* —4F **11**
Chelt Rd. *Chel* —4C **6**
Chelt Wlk. *Chel* —3D **4**
Chequers Bri. *Glos* —4B **20**
Chequers Rd. *Glos* —4B **20**
Cheriton Clo. *Up Hat* —4C **14**
Cherrington Dri. *Abb* —6F **21**
Cherry Av. *Char K* —5D **16**
Cherry Clo. *Hard* —6B **26**
Cherry Gdns. *Huc* —3H **21**
Cherrywood Gdns. *Tuf* —2H **27**
Cherston Ct. *Barn* —3F **21**
Chervil Clo. *Glos* —1C **28**
Cheshire Rd. *Inn* —3F **11**
Chesmann Ct. *Glos* —5A **10**
Chester Rd. *Glos* —3D **20**
Chesterton Ct. *Long* —2B **10**
Chester Wlk. *Chel* —5G **5**
Chestnut Av. *S'hse* —2C **32**
Chestnut Clo. *Qued* —6B **26**
Chestnut La. *Stro* —3A **34**
Chestnut Pl. *Chel* —5E **15**
Chestnut Rd. *Abb* —6F **21**
Chestnuts, The. *Glos* —3G **19**
Chestnut Ter. *Char K* —4B **16**
Chestnut Wlk. *Char K* —4B **16**
Cheviot Clo. *Qued* —5B **26**
Cheviot Rd. *Chel* —3C **6**
Chevril Clo. *Glos* —1C **28**
Cheyney Clo. *Glos* —5C **20**
Chiltern Av. *Bis C* —1D **2**
Chiltern Rd. *Pres* —4C **6**
Chiltern Rd. *Qued* —5B **26**
Chislet Way. *Tuf* —4G **27**
Choirs Clo. *Abb* —5F **21**
Chosen Dri. *C'dwn* —4A **12**
Chosen View Rd. *Chel* —2E **5**
Chosen Way. *Huc* —3G **21**
Christchurch Ct. *Chel* —1D **14**
Christ Chu. Rd. *Chel* —1E **15**
Christ Chu. Ter. *Chel* —5E **5**
Christowe La. *Chel* —2H **15**
Church App. *Bis C* —1E **3**
Churchdown La. *Huc* —4A **22**
Church Dri. *Qued* —4C **26**
Churchfield Rd. *Stro* —4E **35**
Churchfield Rd. *Upton L* —3F **29**
Churchfields. *Bis C* —1F **3**
Churchill Dri. *Char K* —2B **16**
Churchill Dri. *Pain* —5G **31**
Churchill Ind. Est. *Chel* —3G **15**
Churchill Rd. *Chel* —3H **15**
Churchill Rd. *Glos* —4G **19**
Churchill Way. *Pain* —5G **31**
Church La. *Barn* —3E **21**
Church La. *Hard* —6A **26**
Church La. *Pres* —3C **6**
Church La. *S'hse* —3B **32**
Church La. *Shur* —1A **24**
Church La. *Whad* —5H **27**
Church Piece. *Char K* —4C **16**
Church Pl. *Rod* —5B **34**
Church Rise. *Mais* —2D **8**
Church Rd. *Bis C* —1E **3**
Church Rd. *C'dwn* —5B **12**
Church Rd. *L'hptn* —6E **15**
Church Rd. *Leon S* —6B **32**
Church Rd. *Longl* —5D **10**
Church Rd. *Mais* —1D **8**
Church Rd. *St Ma* —1C **14**
Church Rd. *Stro* —4H **33**
Church Rd. *Swin* —1D **4**
Church St. *Char K* —4B **16**
Church St. *Chel* —5G **5**
Church St. *Glos* —2G **19**
Church St. *K Stan* —6D **32**
Church St. *Stro* —3D **34**
Churchview Dri. *Barn* —3E **21**
Church Village. *Qued* —4C **26**
Church Wlk. *Char K* —3C **16**
Church Way. *Glos* —4D **20**
Churn Av. *Chel* —5B **6**
Cicely Way. *Abb* —6G **21**
Circle, The. *Stro* —2D **34**
Cirencester Rd. *Brockw* —1E **31**
Cirencester Rd. *Char K* —2B **16**
Clapham Ct. *Glos* —6A **10**
Clare Ct. *Stro* —3F **35**
Claremont Ct. *Glos* —1A **20**
Claremont Rd. *Glos* —1A **20**
Clarence Pde. *Chel* —6G **5**
Clarence Rd. *Chel* —5H **5**
Clarence Row. *Glos* —1A **20**
Clarence Sq. *Chel* —5H **5**
Clarence St. *Chel* —5G **5**
Clarence St. *Glos* —2H **19**
Clarence Wlk. *Glos* —2H **19**
Clare Pl. *Chel* —2G **15**
Clare St. *Chel* —2G **15**
Clare St. *Glos* —1G **19**
Claridge Clo. *A'dle* —1E **29**
Clarington M. *Chel* —4H **5**
Clark Ct. *Chel* —4B **6**
Clarkia Clo. *C'dwn* —2G **11**
Claudians Way. *Abb* —4F **21**
Clayburn Clo. *H'nam* —4B **8**
Claypits La. *Thr* —6F **35**
Claypits Path. *Chel* —3H **15**
Clearwater Dri. *Qued* —4A **26**
Cleeve Bus. Pk. *Bis C* —4D **2**
Cleeve Clo. *Bis C* —2E **3**
Cleeve Cloud La. *Pres* —4E **7**
Cleevecroft Av. *Bis C* —2F **3**
Cleeve Lake Ct. *Bis C* —1D **2**
Cleevelands Av. *Chel* —2G **5**
Cleevelands Clo. *Chel* —2H **5**
Cleevelands Dri. *Chel* —2H **5**
Cleeveland St. *Chel* —4F **5**
Cleevemount Clo. *Chel* —4A **6**
Cleevemount Rd. *Chel* —4A **6**
Cleeve Rd. *Mat* —1D **28**
Cleeve View Rd. *Chel* —5B **6**
Clegram Rd. *Glos* —4G **19**
Clematis Ct. *Bis C* —2D **2**
Clement Cotts. *Glos* —3B **20**
Clement St. *Glos* —3B **20**
Clevedon Rd. *Glos* —5A **20**
Clevedon Sq. *Chel* —5D **4**
Clifton Rd. *Glos* —3G **19**
Cloisters, The. *Bis C* —1D **2**
Clomoney Way. *Longl* —4E **11**
Close, The. *Chel* —5G **15**
Close, The. *Sthm* —5H **3**
Clover Dri. *Hard* —6B **26**
Clyde Cres. *Chel* —5B **6**
Clyde Rd. *Brockw* —6D **22**
Coal Wharf. *Mais* —2E **9**
Coates Gdns. *S'hse* —2C **32**
Coberley Rd. *Chel* —1A **14**
Coberley Rd. *Tuf* —2H **27**
Cobham Ct. *Chel* —4E **5**
Cobham Rd. *Chel* —4E **5**
Cochran Clo. *C'dwn* —4B **12**
Cold Pool La. *Badg* —6F **13**
Coldray Clo. *Glos* —2C **20**
Cole Av. *Glos* —2E **27**
Colebridge Av. *Glos* —6D **10**
Colerne Dri. *Huc* —4A **22**
Colesbourne Rd. *Chel* —2A **14**
Colin Rd. *Barn* —2E **21**
College Baths Rd. *Chel* —1H **15**
College Ct. *Glos* —1H **19**
College Ga. *Chel* —1H **15**
College Grn. *Glos* —1H **19**
College Lawn. *Chel* —2H **15**
College Pl. Chel —*6G* ***5***
(off Royal Well Pl.)
College Rd. *Chel* —1H **15**
College Rd. *Stro* —2B **34**
College St. *Glos* —1H **19**
College View. *S'hse* —3C **32**
College Yd. Glos —*1G* ***19***
(off College St.)
Colletts Dri. *Chel* —4E **5**
Collingbourne Rd. *Glos* —4B **20**
Collum End Rise. *Chel* —5F **15**
Colne Av. *Chel* —4B **6**
Coltham Clo. *Chel* —1A **16**
Coltham Fields. *Chel* —1A **16**
Coltham Rd. *Chel* —2A **16**
Coltman Clo. *Glos* —2C **20**
Columbia Clo. *Glos* —1A **20**
Columbia St. *Chel* —5H **5**
Colwell Av. *Huc* —2H **21**
Colwyn Dri. *Chel* —3B **14**
Combrook Clo. *Abb* —1F **29**
Commercial Rd. *Glos* —2G **19**
Commercial St. *Chel* —2G **15**
Compton Clo. *C'dwn* —1H **11**
Compton Rd. *Chel* —3E **5**
Concorde Way. *Glos* —4C **20**
Conduit St. *Glos* —4H **19**
Coney Hill Pde. *Glos* —4D **20**
Coney Hill Rd. *Glos* —4C **20**
Conifers, The. *Chel* —4B **6**
Conifers, The. *Glos* —4B **20**
Coniston Rd. *Chel* —2B **14**
Coniston Rd. *Glos* —5D **10**
Constance Clo. *Stro* —5A **34**
Constitution Wlk. *Glos* —2H **19**
Conway Rd. *Huc* —4H **21**
Cook Dri. *Chel* —3A **4**
Cooks La. *Uck* —1A **4**
Cooks Orchard. *Glos* —6B **10**
Coombe Glen La. *Chel* —3A **14**
Coombe Meade. *W'cte* —2G **3**
Coopers Ct. *Brockw* —6D **22**
Coopers Ct. *Char K* —4C **16**

Coopers' Elm. *Qued* —3C **26**
Cooper's View. *Brockw* —6D **22**
Copper Beech Gro. *Qued* —4B **26**
Copperfield Clo. *Mat* —1C **28**
Coppice Ga. *Chel* —2C **4**
Copse, The. *Barn* —4F **21**
Copt Elm Clo. *Char K* —3B **16**
Copt Elm Rd. *Char K* —3B **16**
Coral Clo. *Tuf* —2E **27**
Cordingley Clo. *C'dwn* —5B **12**
Corfe Clo. *Pres* —4D **6**
Coriander Dri. *C'dwn* —3G **11**
Corncroft La. *Mat* —3E **29**
Cornfield Dri. *Bis C* —1D **2**
Cornfield Dri. *Hard* —6B **26**
Cornfields, The. *Bis C* —1C **2**
Cornflower Rd. *Abb* —6F **21**
Cornhill. *Stro* —3D **34**
Cornhill Shopping Cen. Stro —3D ***34***
(off Cornhill)
Cornmeadow Dri. *Chel* —2A **4**
Cornwall Av. *Chel* —5D **4**
Corolin Rd. *Glos* —1E **27**
Coronation Flats. *Chel* —2B **16**
Coronation Gro. *Glos* —1C **20**
Coronation Rd. *Pres* —3C **6**
Coronation Rd. *Stro* —4C **34**
Coronation Sq. *Chel* —5B **4**
Corpus St. *Chel* —1H **15**
Cotswold Edge Bus. Cen. *Glos* —3F **19**
Cotswold Gdns. *Longl* —4E **11**
Cotswold Grn. *S'hse* —2D **32**
Cotswold Mead. *Pain* —6G **31**
Cotswold Rd. *Chel* —4B **6**
Cotswold Rd. *Stro* —2H **33**
Cotswold View. *W'cte* —2G **3**
Cottage Field. *H'nam* —4A **8**
Cottage Rake Av. *Chel* —2F **5**
Cotteswold Rise. *Stro* —3E **35**
Cotteswold Rd. *Glos* —5B **20**
Cotton Clo. *Abb* —6G **21**
Couldridge Rd. *C'dwn* —3H **11**
County Ct. Rd. *Chel* —6G **5**
Courtenay St. *Chel* —4G **5**
Courtenay Vs. *Chel* —4G **5**
Court Farm M. *S'hse* —3A **32**
Courtfield Dri. *Char K* —3C **16**
Courtfield Rd. *Qued* —5B **26**
Court Gdns. *H'std* —5E **19**
Courtiers Dri. *Bis C* —2F **3**
Court Pl. *Glos* —5E **21**
Court Rd. *Brockw* —6D **22**
Court Rd. *Pres* —3D **6**
Court Way. *Stro* —5B **34**
Courtyard, The. Chel —1F ***15***
(off Montpellier St.)
Cousley Clo. *Huc* —4H **21**
Cowle Rd. *Stro* —4E **35**
Cowley Clo. *Chel* —2B **14**
Cowley Rd. *Tuf* —2H **27**
Cowlsmead. *Shur* —1A **24**
Cowper Rd. *Chel* —6B **4**
Cowslip Meadow. *W'cte* —2G **3**
Coxmore Clo. *Huc* —4H **21**
Cox's Way. *Abb* —5H **21**
Crab Tree Pl. *Chel* —4F **5**
Cranford Clo. *W'cte* —2H **3**
Cranham Clo. *Abb* —6F **21**
Cranham La. *C'dwn* —6C **12**
Cranham Rd. *Chel* —6A **6**
Cranwell Clo. *Mat* —1D **28**
Craven Dri. *C'dwn* —3H **11**
Credon Rd. *Glos* —2F **21**
Crescent Clo. *S'hse* —4B **32**
Crescentdale. *Long* —4B **10**
Crescent Pl. *Chel* —6G **5**
Crescent Rd. *S'hse* —4B **32**
Crescent Ter. *Chel* —6G **5**
Crescent, The. *Brockw* —5D **22**
Crest Way. *Huc* —2G **21**
Criftycraft La. *C'dwn* —6B **12**
Crippetts Rd. *L'hptn* —2D **24**
Crispin Clo. *Longl* —3D **10**
Croft Av. *Char K* —4B **16**
Croft Clo. *C'dwn* —5C **12**
Croft Dri. *Char K* —4B **16**
Croft Gdns. *Char K* —5C **16**
Croft La. *Chel* —3G **15**
Croft Pde. *Char K* —4C **16**
Croft Rd. *Char K* —4B **16**
Croft St. *Chel* —3F **15**
Croft, The. *Pain* —5H **31**
Croft Thorne Clo. *Up Hat* —4C **14**
Cromwell Rd. *Chel* —4A **6**
Cromwell St. *Glos* —2H **19**
Cross Keys La. *Glos* —1H **19**
Crowfield *W'cte* —1G **3**
Crown Clo. *Bis C* —2E **3**
Crown Ct. *K Stan* —6D **32**
Crown Dri. *Bis C* —2E **3**
Crummock Wlk. *Chel* —3C **14**
Crypt Ct. *Tuf* —2F **27**
Crythan Wlk. *Up Hat* —4C **14**
Cudnall St. *Char K* —2B **16**
Culross Clo. *Chel* —3H **5**
Cumberland Cres. *Chel* —6D **4**
Cumming Ct. *Chel* —3B **6**
Curlew Rd. *A'dle* —5D **20**
Curtis Haywood Dri. *Qued* —4B **26**
Cutler Rd. *Stro* —2E **35**
Cutsdean Clo. *Bis C* —1C **2**
Cutsdean Rd. *Bis C* —1C **2**

Daffodil Clo. *Abb* —6F **21**
Daffodil St. *Chel* —1G **15**
Dagmar Rd. *Chel* —2F **15**
Dainty St. *Glos* —4A **20**
Daisy Bank. *Stro* —4F **35**
Daisybank Rd. *L'hptn* —1G **25**
Dale Clo. *Glos* —6A **20**
Dale Wlk. *Bis C* —2F **3**
Damson Clo. *Abb* —1F **29**
Dancey Rd. *C'dwn* —3G **11**
Dane Clo. *Longl* —4D **10**
Daniels Ind. Est. *Dud* —5A **34**
Daniels Rd. *Stro* —3G **35**
Darell Clo. *Qued* —6C **26**
Dark La. *Rod* —5C **34**
Dark La. *Swin V* —6A **2**
Dart Rd. *Chel* —4C **6**
Darwin Clo. *Chel* —1H **13**
Darwin Rd. *Glos* —6B **20**
Davallia Dri. *Up Hat* —4C **14**
Daventry Ter. *Glos* —3A **20**
David French Ct. *Chel* —4D **14**
Dawes, The. *Qued* —5C **26**
Daylesford Clo. *Chel* —1A **14**
Deacon Clo. *Chel* —2C **14**
Deacons Pl. *Bis C* —3E **3**
Deakin Clo. *Swin* —6A **2**
Deans Ct. *Chel* —2C **14**
Dean's Ter. *Glos* —6H **9**
Dean's Wlk. *Glos* —6H **9**
(in two parts)
Dean's Way. *Bis C* —2E **3**
Dean's Way. *Glos* —6H **9**
Deep St. *Pres* —3C **6**
Deerhurst Clo. *Abb* —1F **29**
Deerhurst Pl. *Qued* —4B **26**
Deer Pk. Rd. *Huc* —2H **21**
De Ferriers Wlk. *Chel* —5A **4**
Delabere Rd. *Bis C* —3F **3**
Dell, The. *Barn* —4F **21**
Delmont Gro. *Stro* —2D **34**
Delphinium Dri. *Bis C* —2D **2**
Denbigh Rd. *Chel* —3B **14**
Denham Clo. *Tuf* —4F **27**
Denham Clo. *W'cte* —2H **3**
Denley Clo. *Bis C* —3E **3**
Denmark Ct. *Glos* —6B **10**
Denmark Rd. *Glos* —6A **10**
Derby Ct. *Glos* —2B **20**
Derby Rd. *Glos* —3B **20**
Derwent Clo. *Brockw* —6D **22**
Derwent Wlk. *Chel* —2C **14**
Desford Clo. *Abb* —6G **21**
Detmore Clo. *Char K* —4E **17**
Devereaux Cres. *Ebl* —3F **33**
Devereaux Rd. *Ebl* —3F **33**
Devon Av. *Chel* —6C **4**
Devonshire St. *Chel* —5F **5**
Dewey Clo. *W'cte* —2G **3**
Dianas Clo. *Abb* —5G **21**
Dickens Clo. *Glos* —6A **20**
Didbrook M. *Abb* —1F **29**
Dill Av. *Chel* —3B **4**
Dimore Clo. *Hard* —6A **26**
Dinas Clo. *Chel* —3C **14**
Dinas Rd. *Chel* —3C **14**
Dinglewell. *Huc* —3G **21**
Dinley St. *Glos* —3A **20**
Discovery Rd. *Abb* —5G **21**
Distel Clo. *Chel* —2F **5**
Dodington Clo. *Barn* —4E **21**
Dog Bark La. *Swin* —1D **4**
Dog La. *B'hm* —5H **23**
Dombey Bungalows. *Glos* —1F **27**
Dora Wlk. *Glos* —4A **20**
Dorchester Ct. *Chel* —3F **15**
Dormer Rd. *Chel* —3C **4**
Dorney Rd. *Glos* —4G **19**
Dorrington Wlk. *Chel* —5A **4**
Dorrit Clo. *Glos* —5A **20**
Dorset Av. *Chel* —5D **4**
Douro Rd. *Chel* —6E **5**
Doverdale Dri. *Longl* —5E **11**
Dover Hay. *Up Hat* —3C **14**
Dowding Way. *C'dwn* —4B **12**
Downfield. *Stro* —2A **34**
Downfield Rd. *Stro* —3A **34**
Down Hatherley La. *Dwn H* —1A **12**
Downton Rd. *S'hse* —4B **32**
Downy Clo. *Qued* —3B **26**
Dowty Rd. *Chel* —5B **4**
Dozule Clo. *Leon S* —6C **32**
Drake Clo. *C'dwn* —2G **11**
Drakes Pl. *Chel* —6E **5**
Drapers Ct. *W'cte* —2G **3**
Draycott Rd. *Chel* —1B **14**
Drayton Clo. *Swin V* —2E **5**
Drayton Way. *Glos* —6D **20**
Drews Clo. *C'dwn* —5B **12**
Drews Ct. *C'dwn* —5B **12**
Drivemoor. *A'dle* —2E **29**
Druids Clo. *Glos* —4D **20**
Druids La. *Glos* —4D **20**
Druids Oak. *Qued* —5C **26**
Ducie St. *Glos* —4A **20**
Duckworth Clo. *Chel* —4G **15**
Dudbridge Hill. *Stro* —4A **34**
Dudbridge Meadow. *Dud* —5A **34**
Dudbridge Rd. *Dud* —4A **34**
Duderstadt Clo. *Stro* —2A **34**
Duke of Beaufort Ct. *Glos* —6G **19**
Dukeries, The. *Glos* —1G **19**
Duke St. *Chel* —6A **6**
Dumbleton Gro. *Red T* —3G **13**
Dunalley Pde. *Chel* —4G **5**
(in two parts)
Dunalley St. *Chel* —5G **5**
Dunbar Clo. *Chel* —3A **4**
Duncroft Rd. *Huc* —2G **21**
Dunlin Clo. *Qued* —4A **26**
Dunstan Glen. *C'dwn* —5C **12**
Dunster Clo. *Chel* —4A **4**
Dunster Clo. *Tuf* —4E **27**
Dunster Gdns. *Chel* —4A **4**
Dunster Gro. *Chel* —4A **4**
Dunster Rd. *Chel* —4A **4**
Durand Clo. *Longl* —3D **10**
Durham Clo. *Chel* —4D **14**
Durham Rd. *Glos* —3D **20**
Dynevor St. *Glos* —4A **20**

Eagle Way. *A'dle* —6D **20**
Eardisland Rd. *Tuf* —3H **27**
E. Approach Dri. *Chel* —3A **6**
Eastbrook Rd. *Glos* —3D **20**
Eastbrook Rd. Trad. Est. *Glos* —3D **20**
Eastcott Way. *C'dwn* —3H **11**
E. Court M. *Char K* —4C **16**
East Ct. Vs. *Char K* —4D **16**
East Dri. *Ebl* —3F **33**
E. End Rd. *Char K* —4C **16**
Eastern Av. *Glos* —5B **20**
Eastern Av. Trad. Est. *Glos* —3C **20**
E. Gable. *W'cte* —2H **3**
Eastgate Mkt. Glos —2H ***19***
(off Forum, The)
Eastgate Shopping Cen. *Glos* —2H **19**
Eastgate St. *Glos* —2H **19**
Eastville Clo. *Glos* —3C **20**
Ebley By-Pass. *S'hse & Dud* —4D **32**
Ebley Ind. Est. *Ebl* —4G **33**
Ebley Ind. Pk. *Ebl* —4G **33**
Ebley Rd. *S'hse* —4D **32**
Ebor Rd. *Glos* —2D **20**
Ebrington Clo. *Barn* —3E **21**
Edendale App. *Chel* —1H **13**
Edendale Rd. *Chel* —6A **4**
Edge Rd. *Pain* —5G **31**
Edgeworth Clo. *Abb* —6F **21**
Edinburgh Pl. *Chel* —5B **4**
Edward St. *Chel* —2G **15**
Edward Wilson Ho. *Chel* —4B **4**
Edwy Pde. *Glos* —6H **9**
Elderberry Mews. *C'dwn* —3G **11**
Eldersfield Clo. *Qued* —3B **26**
Elderwood Way. *Tuf* —2F **27**
Eldon Av. *Chel* —6B **6**
Eldon Rd. *Chel* —6A **6**
Eldorado Cres. *Chel* —6E **5**
Eldorado Rd. *Chel* —6D **4**
Eliot Clo. *Glos* —1F **27**
Ellenborough Rd. *Bis C* —3F **3**
Ellesmere Clo. *Huc* —3G **21**
Ellesmere Gro. *Chel* —3E **15**
Elliott Pl. *Chel* —2C **14**
Ellison Clo. *Abb* —5H **21**
Ellison Rd. *Chel* —5B **4**
Elmbridge Rd. *Glos* —1D **20**
Elm Clo. *Chel* —4E **5**
Elm Clo. *K Stan* —6D **32**
Elm Clo. *Pres* —2B **6**
Elm Dri. *Brockw* —5C **22**
Elmfield Av. *Chel* —3F **5**
Elmfield Rd. *Chel* —3F **5**
Elm Garden Dri. *Red T* —2F **13**
Elmgrove Est. *Hard* —6B **26**
Elmgrove Rd. *Huc* —4H **21**
Elmgrove Rd. E. *Hard* —6B **26**
Elmgrove Rd. W. *Hard* —6A **26**
Elmira Rd. *Glos* —1A **28**
Elmlea Rd. *K Stan* —6D **32**
Elmleaze. *Glos* —6D **10**
Elmore La. *Qued* —3A **26**
(in two parts)
Elm Rd. *Stro* —2H **33**
Elms Rd. *S'hse* —2B **32**
Elms, The. *S'hse* —2B **32**
Elmstone St. *Chel* —5F **5**
Elm St. *Chel* —4E **5**
Eltham Lawn. *Chel* —1E **15**
Emerald Clo. *Tuf* —2F **27**
Emmanuel Gdns. *Chel* —3G **15**
Emperor Clo. *Chel* —5A **4**
Empire Way. *Glos* —6E **19**
Enborne Clo. *Tuf* —4G **27**
Ennerdale Av. *Longl* —4D **10**
Ennerdale Rd. *Chel* —2B **14**
Enterprise Way. *Chel* —4E **5**
Epney Rd. *Tuf & L'ney* —2F **27**
Erin Pk. *Stro* —5B **34**
Ermin Pk. *Brockw* —5C **22**
Erminster Dri. *Huc* —4H **21**
Ermin St. *Brockw* —5B **22**
Eros Clo. *Stro* —5B **34**
Essex Av. *Chel* —5D **4**
Essex Clo. *C'dwn* —1H **11**
Essex Pl. *Chel* —6H **5**
Estcourt Clo. *Glos* —5B **10**
Estcourt Rd. *Glos* —5A **10**
Etheldene Rd. *Stro* —2G **33**
Etheridge Pl. *Glos* —2C **20**
Ettington Clo. *Chel* —4A **4**
Evans Wlk. *Mat* —1C **28**
Evelyn Clo. *Char K* —4H **15**
Evelyn Ct. *Chel* —1F **15**
Evenlode Av. *Chel* —5B **6**
Evenlode Rd. *Tuf* —4G **27**
Everest Rd. *Chel* —5H **15**
Evesham Rd. *Bis C* —1E **3**
Evesham Rd. *Chel & Pres* —5H **5**
Evington Ct. *Chel* —5B **4**
Evington Rd. *Chel* —5B **4**
Ewens Rd. *Char K* —1B **16**
Ewlyn Rd. *Chel* —3G **15**
Ewlyn Ter. *Chel* —3G **15**
Exmouth Ct. *Chel* —2G **15**
Exmouth St. *Chel* —2G **15**
Eynon Clo. *Chel* —3F **15**

Fairfield Av. *Chel* —3G **15**
Fairfield Pde. *Chel* —3G **15**
Fairfield Pk. Rd. *Chel* —3G **15**
Fairfield Rd. *Chel* —3G **15**
Fairfield St. *Chel* —3G **15**
Fairfield Wlk. *Chel* —3G **15**
Fairford Way. *Glos* —4C **20**
Fairhaven Av. *Brockw* —5C **22**
Fairhaven Rd. *Chel* —3G **15**
Fairhaven St. *Chel* —3G **15**
Fairmile Gdns. *Long* —4A **10**
Fairmount Rd. *Chel* —6C **4**
Fairview Clo. *Chel* —6H **5**
Fairview Rd. *Chel* —5H **5**
Fairview St. *Chel* —5H **5**
Fairwater Pk. *Barn* —2E **21**
Falcon Clo. *Inn* —3D **10**
Faldo Clo. *Abb* —6G **21**
Falfield Rd. *Tuf* —2F **27**
Falkland Pl. *Chel* —4A **4**
Falkner St. *Glos* —3A **20**
(in two parts)
Faraday Clo. *Glos* —4A **20**
Faringdon Rd. *Chel* —2A **14**
Far Leazes. *Stro* —3E **35**
Farleigh Clo. *Char K* —3D **16**
Farm Clo. *Chel* —4B **4**
Farmfield Rd. *Chel* —4C **14**
Farmhill Cres. *Stro* —1A **34**
Farmhill La. *Stro* —2A **34**
Farmington Clo. *Abb* —6F **21**
Farmington Rd. *Chel* —1B **14**
Farm La. *Chel* —5E **15**

Farm La. Shur —2A 24
Farm M. Glos —4H 19
Farm St. Glos —3H 19
Farrant Av. C'dwn —3H 11
Farriers End. Qued —3C 26
Farriers Reach. Bis C —1C 2
Farr's La. Stro —3D 34
Far Sandfield. C'dwn —4B 12
Farthing Croft. H'nam —5A 8
Far Westrip. Wtrp —2F 33
Fauconberg Rd. Chel —6F 5
Fawkes Pl. Stro —3D 34
Fawley Dri. Pres —3D 6
Fennel Clo. A'dle —1E 29
Fennells View. Stro —1F 35
Ferndale Clo. Glos —3C 10
Ferndales Clo. Up Hat —4C 14
Fern Lawn. A'dle —3E 29
Fernleigh Cres. Up Hat —3B 14
Ferry Gdns. Qued —4A 26
Festival Rd. S'hse —3B 32
Fiddler's Grn. La. Chel —5A 4
Fieldcote Dri. Huc —4H 21
Field Ct. Dri. Qued —5B 26
Field Ct. Gdns. Qued —6B 26
Fielden. A'dle —2E 29
Field End. C'dwn —2A 12
Fieldfare. A'dle —6E 21
Fieldgate Rd. Bis C —1F 3
Field Rd. Rod —4B 34
Field Rd. Stro —4E 35
Field Ter. Rod —4C 34
Filbert Clo. A'dle —1E 29
Filton Way. Glos —4C 20
Finchcroft Ct. Pres —3E 7
Finchcroft La. Pres —4D 6
Finchmoor M. Long —4A 10
Finch Rd. Inn —3E 11
Finlay Pl. Glos —6A 20
Finlay Rd. Glos —1H 27
Finstock Clo. Chel —1C 14
Fircroft Clo. Huc —3G 21
Fircroft Rd. Long —3A 10
Firethorne Clo. Glos —3C 10
Firgrove Wlk. Chel —2H 13
Firs, The. Glos —6B 10
Firs, The. Swin —6A 2
Fir Tree Clo. Chel —3B 6
Firwood Dri. Tuf —2H 27
Fishers La. Chel —5H 5
Fishers Way. K'ct —6B 34
Fisher Wlk. Chel —3C 4
Flaxley Rd. Tuf —2G 27
Flecker's Dri. Chel —2C 14
Fleming Clo. Glos —3D 10
Flint Rd. Chel —3B 14
Florida Dri. Pres —3D 6
Flower Way. Longl —5C 10
Foley Clo. Tuf —3G 27
Folland Av. Huc —5A 22
Folly Ct. Stro —1E 35
Folly La. Chel —3G 5
Folly La. Stro —3D 34
Folly Rise. Stro —1E 35
Forest View Rd. Tuf —3H 27
Forsyte Way. Glos —4C 20
Forsythia Clo. C'dwn —2H 11
Fortina Clo. Chel —2F 5
Fort View Ter. Stro —4H 33
Forty Acre La. Stro —3H 35
Forum, The. Glos —2H 19
(off Market Way)
Fosse Clo. Abb —5F 21
Foster Clo. Bis C —1F 3
Fountain Sq. Glos —1G 19
Fox Clo. Abb —6H 21
Fox Clo. Stro —2G 33
Foxcote. Glos —4C 10
Fox Elms Rd. Tuf —3H 27
Foxglove Clo. Abb —6F 21
Foxgrove Dri. Chel —6B 6
Foxleigh Cres. Glos —4F 11
Foxmoor. Bis C —1D 2
Foxmoor La. Ebl —3F 33
Foxtail Clo. Glos —6B 20
Foxwell Dri. Huc —3G 21
Frampton M. Red T —2G 13
Frampton Rd. Glos —4G 19
Francis St. Chel —2G 15
Frank Brookes Rd. Chel —3D 4
Fretherne Rd. Tuf —2G 27
Frewin Clo. Chel —5A 4
Friars Clo. Chel —4E 15
Friary Rd. Abb —5F 21
Friday St. Pain —5H 31
Frobisher M. C'dwn —1G 11
Frog Furlong La. Dwn H & Inn —1F 11
Frome Av. Stro —4B 34
Frome Gdns. Stro —4H 33
Frome Pk. Rd. Stro —4B 34
Fulbrook Clo. Chel —2A 4
Fullers Ct. Glos —1G 19
Furlong La. Bis C —2D 2
Furlong Rd. Glos —4H 19
Furze Croft. Qued —6C 26
Furze, The. Glos —1B 28

Gable Point. W'cte —2G 3
Gadshill Rd. Char K —6C 16
Gainsborough Dri. Tuf —3F 27
Gallagher Retail Pk. Swin —2C 4
Gallops La. Pres —4E 7
Gambier Parry Gdns. Glos —5A 10
Gambles La. W'cte —3H 3
Gannet Clo. Brockw —6D 22
Gannicox Rd. Stro —3B 34
Gara Clo. Swin —2C 4
Gardener's La. Chel —3F 5
Gardeners Way. K Stan —6D 32
Gardenia Gro. Up Hat —4C 14
Garden Rd. Char K —5C 16
Gardens, The. Chel —3H 5
Garden Way. Longl —5C 10
Gardiners Clo. C'dwn —3A 12
Garnalls Rd. Mat —1D 28
Garside Pl. Chel —4F 15
Gatcombe Clo. Bis C —2D 2
Gatmeres Rd. Mat —2D 28
Gatton Way. Huc —2G 21
Gazelle Clo. Qued —3C 26
Genista Way. Up Hat —4C 14
George Readings Way. Chel —3C 4
George St. Glos —1A 20
George St. Stro —3D 34
George Whitfield Clo. Mat —1D 28
Georgian Clo. A'dle —2F 29
Gere Clo. Tuf —3G 27
Gibson Clo. Stro —3G 35
Gibson Rd. Inn —2F 11
Giffard Way. Chel —5G 15
Gifford Clo. Longl —4D 10
Gilbert Rd. Longl —4D 10
Gilberts La. Brook —6A 28
Gilbert Ward Ct. Char K —4B 16
Gilder Rd. Bis C —3F 3
Gilders Paddock. Bis C —1E 3
Giles Cox. Qued —5C 26
Gilpin Av. Huc —2G 21
Gimson Clo. Tuf —3G 27
Gladiator Clo. Brockw —6D 22
Gladstone Rd. Char K —4B 16
Gladstone Rd. Glos —5F 19
Glamorgan Rd. Chel —3B 14
Glebe Farm Ct. Up Hat —4C 14
Glebe Rd. Pres —3C 6
Glencairn Av. Tuf —4F 27
Glencairn Ct. Chel —1D 14
Glencairn Pk. Rd. Chel —1D 14
Glen Ct. S'hse —2C 32
Glendower Clo. C'dwn —1G 11
Glenfall St. Chel —5H 5
Glenfall Way. Char K —3C 16
Glenlea Gro. Up Hat —4C 14
Glen Pk. Cres. K'ct —6B 34
Glensanda Ct. Chel —1G 15
Glenthorne Clo. S'hse —1C 32
Glenville Pde. Huc —4H 21
Glevum Clo. Longl —5C 10
Glevum Ct. Chel —5A 4
(off Marsland Rd.)
Glevum Shopping Cen. A'dle —1E 29
Glevum Way. A'dle —1F 29
Gloucester & Cheltenham Airport. Chel (Staverton) —1B 12
Gloucester Cotts. Chel —5E 5
Gloucester Grn. Barn —1E 21
Gloucester Northern By-Pass. Glos & Inn —5F 9
Gloucester Pl. Chel —6H 5
Gloucester Retail Pk. Glos —3D 20
Gloucester Rd. Chel —1H 13
Gloucester Rd. Pain —4H 31
Gloucester Rd. S'hse —1C 32
Gloucester St. Pain —4H 31
Gloucester St. Stro —3D 34
Gloucester Trad. Est. Huc —5A 22
Glynbridge Ct. Glos —4A 20
Glynbridge Gdns. Chel —2C 4
Glyndthorpe Gro. Up Hat —4B 14
Glynfield Rise. Ebl —3F 33
Glynrosa Rd. Char K —4C 16
Goddard Way. Tuf —3G 27
Godfrey Clo. Chel —2D 14
Godwin Clo. Chel —5A 6
Goldcrest Ct. S'hse —2C 32
Golden Clo. Tuf —3F 27
Golden Miller Rd. Chel —2F 5
Golden Vale. C'dwn —3A 12
Golden Valley By-Pass. Glos & Chel —4G 11
Golden Valley Interchange. Chel —2E 13
Goldsborough Clo. Glos —4C 20
Goldsmith Rd. Chel —5B 4
Golf Club La. Brockw —1B 30
Goodmoor Cres. C'dwn —3H 11
Goodridge Av. Glos —2D 26
Goodwin Ct. Glos —4H 19
Goodyere St. Glos —3A 20
(in two parts)
Gordon Clo. H'nam —4B 8
Gordon Rd. Chel —4F 15
Gorse Clo. Abb —1G 29
Goshawk Gdns. Qued —2C 26
Goss Wood Corner. Qued —5B 26
Gotherington La. Bis C —1F 3
Gouda Way. Glos —6H 9
Goy Ct. Glos —5H 19
Grafton Rd. Chel —2F 15
Grafton Rd. Glos —6C 10
Graham Gdns. Glos —6C 10
Graham Pl. Chel —4A 4
Grange Dri. Bis C —2E 3
Grange Rd. Tuf —3F 27
Granger Rd. Glos —2D 20
Grange View. Upl —2D 34
Grange Wlk. Char K —4C 16
Granley Clo. Chel —1C 14
Granley Dri. Chel —1C 14
Granley Gdns. Chel —1C 14
Granley Rd. Chel —1C 14
Granville St. Chel —5F 5
Granville St. Glos —5F 19
Grasby Clo. Barn —4F 21
Grasmere Rd. Chel —2C 14
Grasmere Rd. Glos —5D 10
Gratton Rd. Chel —2F 15
Gratton St. Chel —2G 15
Gravel Pit La. Pres —2D 6
Gravel Wlk. Sthm —5H 3
Gravney Ct. Chel —3B 4
Gray Clo. Inn —2F 11
Grayling Clo. Abb —6F 21
Greatfield Dri. Char K —4A 16
Greatfield La. Up Hat —3A 14
(in two parts)
Gt. Norwood St. Chel —2F 15
Gt. Western Ct. Glos —2B 20
Gt. Western Rd. Chel —5F 5
Gt. Western Rd. Glos —1A 20
Gt. Western Ter. Chel —5F 5
Grebe Clo. A'dle —6D 20
Green Acre. Brockw —6D 22
Green Bank. Brockw —1D 30
Green Clo. Brockw —1D 30
Green Gdns. Brockw —1D 30
Greenhill Ct. Tuf —2E 27
Greenhill Dri. Glos —2D 26
Greenhills Clo. Chel —4H 15
Greenhills Rd. Char K —4A 16
Greenhouse La. Pain —6H 31
Greenings, The. Up Hat —4C 14
Green La. Brockw —4F 23
Green La. C'dwn —5B 12
Green La. Hard —6A 26
Green La. Huc —5H 21
Green Meadow Bank. Bis C —1D 2
Green St. Brockw —1C 30
Green St. S'hse —2C 32
Green, The. Bis C —2E 3
Green, The. C'dwn —6B 12
Green, The. H'nam —4A 8
Green, The. K Stan —6D 32
Green, The. Sel —6H 33
Green, The. Uck —1A 4
Green Way. Brockw —6D 22
Greenway. W'cte —2G 3
Greenway Clo. Shur —2A 24
Greenway La. Char K —2B 16
Greenway La. Shur & Ull —2A 24
Greenwood Clo. Huc —5A 22
Grenadier Clo. Abb —5G 21
Grenadier Rd. Chel —3B 4
Grenville Clo. C'dwn —1G 11
Greville Ct. Chel —1C 14
Grevil Rd. Chel —3C 4
Greyfriars. Glos —2H 19
Greyhound Gdns. Longl —4E 11
Griffin Mill Est. Stro —6E 35
Griffiths Av. Chel —1C 14
Griffon Clo. Qued —2C 26
Grimwade Clo. Chel —6C 4
Grisedale Clo. Longl —4D 10
Grist Mill Clo. Chel —2A 4
Grosvenor Houses. Glos —1A 20
Grosvenor Pl. S. Chel —6H 5
Grosvenor Rd. Glos —1C 20
Grosvenor Rd. S'hse —1C 32
Grosvenor St. Chel —6H 5
Grosvenor Ter. Chel —6H 5
Grove Cres. Barn —2D 20
Grovefield Way. Chel —2G 13
Grovelands. Glos —3F 21
Grovelands Clo. Char K —3C 16
Grove Pk. Rd. Upl —2D 34
Grove Rd. C'dwn —4G 11
Grove St. Chel —5F 5
Grove St. Glos —3A 20
Grove, The. Chel —6B 6
Grove, The. Ebl —4G 33
Grove, The. L'dwn —1E 15
Grove, The. Sel —6H 33
Guestriss Cotts. Chel —2G 5
Guildings Way. K Stan —5D 32
Guinea St. Glos —6A 10
Guise Av. Brockw —1E 31
Guise Clo. Qued —5C 26
Gunhouse La. Bow —5E 35
Gurney Av. Tuf —3G 27
Gwernant Rd. Chel —3C 14
Gyde Rd. Pain —4H 31

Hadow Way. Qued —5C 26
Hadrians Way. Abb —4F 21
Hailes Rd. Glos —4E 21
Hale La. Pain —5H 31
Hales Clo. Chel —6B 6
Hale's Rd. Chel —1A 16
Halland Rd. Chel —4G 15
Hallmead Clo. Chel —2A 4
Hall Rd. Chel —5G 15
Hambrook St. Char K —2C 16
Hambrook Ter. Char K —3C 16
Hambutts Dri. Pain —5G 31
Hambutts Mead. Pain —5G 31
Ham Clo. Char K —2D 16
Hamer St. Glos —2C 20
Hamilton St. Char K —2B 16
Hammond Ct. Barn —2E 21
Hammond Ct. Chel —2H 15
Hammond Way. Barn —2E 21
Hampden Way. Glos —2H 19
Hampton Clo. Huc —4A 22
Hampton Clo. L'hptn —4D 14
Hampton Pl. C'dwn —1H 11
Ham Rd. Char K —2D 16
Ham Sq. Char K —2D 16
Hanman Rd. Glos —4A 20
Hanna Ct. Chel —5G 5
Hannah Pl. Inn —2F 11
Hannam Clo. Chel —5G 15
Hanover Ct. Chel —2E 15
Hanover Pde. Chel —4G 5
Hanover St. Chel —4G 5
Hanover Way. C'dwn —2G 11
Harbury M. Glos —3B 20
Hardy Rd. Bis C —1E 3
Harebell Pl. Abb —6E 21
Hare La. Glos —1H 19
(in two parts)
Harewood Clo. Tuf —4F 27
Harper Rd. Stro —2H 33
Harpfield Clo. Bis C —2E 3
Harpfield Rd. Bis C —2E 3
Harp Hill. Char K —6B 6
Harrington Dri. Chel —2B 14
Harris Clo. C'dwn —4B 12
Harrison Pl. Tuf —3F 27
Harrison Rd. Shur —1A 24
Harry Yates Way. Chel —3A 4
Hartbury Clo. Chel —4A 4
Harthurstfield Farm Cvn. Pk. Chel —1H 13
Hartington Rd. Glos —5F 19
Hartland Rd. Glos —5A 20
Hartlebury Way. Char K —3D 16
Hartley Clo. Char K —5A 16
Harvesters View. Bis C —1C 2
Harvest Gro. Chel —2A 4
Harvest Way. Qued —6C 26
Harvey Clo. Pod —6F 19
Harwell Clo. Tuf —4G 27
Hasfield Clo. Qued —4B 26
Haslette Way. Up Hat —4B 14
Hatfield Rd. Glos —4B 20
Hathaway Clo. Glos —1F 27

Hatherley Brake. Chel —2B 14
Hatherley Ct. Chel —2E 15
Hatherley Ct. Rd. Chel —2E 15
Hatherley Ga. Chel —2E 15
Hatherley La. Chel —1H 13
Hatherley Rd. Chel —3A 14
Hatherley Rd. Glos —4A 20
Hatherley St. Chel —2E 15
Havan Rd. S'hse —4B 32
Havelock Rd. Huc —3H 21
Haven Ct. Glos —6D 10
Haven Pk. Up Hat —3A 14
Haver, The. Char K —2C 16
Hawcombe M. Up Hat —3C 14
Haweswater Rd. Chel —3C 14
Hawk Clo. A'dle —6E 21
Hawkswood Rd. Chel —4E 15
Hawthorn Dri. W'cte —2G 3
Hawthorne Av. Glos —5D 20
Hawthorne Dri. C'dwn —3H 11
Hawthornes, The. Up Hat —3A 14
Hawthorn Rise. Stro —2G 33
Hawthorn Rd. Chel —4B 4
Haycroft Clo. Bis C —1D 2
Haycroft Dri. Mat —3E 29
Haydale Gdns. Longl —4D 10
Hayden Rd. Chel —2B 4
Hayes Ct. Long —3A 10
Hayes Rd. Chel —5B 6
Hayfield Way. Bis C —1C 2
Haylea Rd. Bis C —1C 2
Haymes Dri. C Hill —4H 3
Haymes Rd. C Hill —4H 3
Hay's Cotts. Chel —3H 15
Haywards La. Chel —1B 16
Hayward's Rd. Chel —2A 16
Haywicks La. Hard —5A 26
Hazebrouck Clo. Chel —2B 14
Hazel Clo. Glos —4C 10
Hazelcroft. C'dwn —3A 12
Hazels, The. Abb —4F 21
Hazelwood Clo. Chel —4E 15
Hazledean Rd. Chel —3A 4
Hazlitt Croft. Chel —3A 4
Headlam Clo. Tuf —4G 27
Heapey Clo. Chel —5A 4
Hearne Clo. Char K —3C 16
Hearne Rd. Char K —3C 16
Heathdean Rd. C'dwn —3G 11
Heather Av. Abb —1G 29
Heather Clo. Stro —6B 34
Heathfield Rd. Stro —1B 34
Heathville Rd. Glos —1A 20
Heazle Pl. Stro —2D 34
Hebden Clo. Brockw —6E 23
Hedgerow, The. Longl —5C 10
Helens Clo. Chel —4A 4
Hembury Clo. Hard —6A 26
Hemmingsdale Rd. H'std —2F 19
Hemming Way. Bis C —2E 3
Hempsted La. H'std —5E 19
Hendingham Clo. Tuf —3E 27
Hendre M. Chel —6F 5
Henley Ct. Stro —2G 33
Henley Pl. Glos —6G 19
Henley Rd. Chel —4A 4
Henrietta St. Chel —5G 5
Henry Rd. Glos —6A 10
Henry Ryder Clo. Abb —5G 21
Henry St. Glos —1A 20
Herbert St. Glos —3B 20
Hereford Pl. Chel —5F 5
Hermitage St. Chel —2G 15
Heron Clo. Chel —2B 14
Heron Way. A'dle —6D 20
Hertford Rd. Bis C —1F 3
Hester's Way La. Chel —3A 4
Hester's Way Rd. Chel —4A 4
Hethersett Rd. Glos —3B 20
Hetton Gdns. Chel —3B 16
Hewlett Pl. Chel —6H 5
Hewlett Rd. Chel —6H 5
Hickley Gdns. Brockw —5D 22
Hicks Beach Rd. Chel —4A 4
Hidcote Av. Up Hat —4D 14
Highbank Pk. Long —5A 10
Highbury La. Chel —6H 5
Highbury M. Chel —1A 16
Highclere Rd. Qued —3B 26
Highfield Pl. Glos —4C 20
Highfield Rd. Glos —4C 20
Highfield Rd. Stro —4F 35
Highgrove, The. Bis C —2D 2
Highgrove Way. C'dwn —2G 11
Highland Rd. Chel —5H 15
Highliffe Dri. Qued —4D 26
High Orchard St. Glos —3G 19
High St. Cheltenham, Chel —5F 5
(in two parts)
High St. Gloucester, Glos —4A 20
High St. King's Stanley, K Stan —6D 32
High St. Prestbury, Pres —3D 6
High St. Stonehouse, S'hse —2C 32
High St. Stroud, Stro —3D 34
High St. Upton St Leonards, Upton L —3F 29
High View. H'std —5D 18
Highwood Av. Chel —3F 15
Highworth Rd. Glos —5A 20
Hildyard Clo. Hard —6B 26
Hillands Dri. Chel —5G 15
Hillary Rd. Chel —5H 15
Hillborough Rd. Tuf —2H 27
Hillclose Est. Stro —6B 34
Hillcot Clo. Qued —4B 26
Hill Cotts. Glos —6A 10
Hill Ct. Rd. Chel —3H 5
Hill Crest. H'nam —4A 8
Hillcrest Rd. Stro —2G 33
Hillfield. Chel —6C 4
Hillfield. Stro —3A 34
Hillfield Ct. Glos —1B 20
Hillfield Ct. Rd. Glos —6B 10
Hill Hay Rd. Mat —2D 28
Hillier Clo. Stro —1E 35
Hillier Dri. Up Hat —5C 14
Hill Rd. Glos —1A 28
Hillside Clo. Chel —2D 14
Hillside Clo. W'cte —2H 3
Hillside Gdns. W'cte —2H 3
Hill, The. Stro —3C 34
Hill Top Clo. Stro —3F 35
Hill Top Rd. Chel —3G 5
Hillview Av. Brockw —5C 22
Hill View Cotts. Tuf —3H 27
Hillview Dri. Huc —3G 21
Hillview Rd. Chel —5C 6
Hillview Rd. Huc —3G 21
Hilton Clo. H'std —5E 19
Hine Gdns. Chel —4A 6
Hinton Rd. Glos —5A 10
Hisnams Field. Bis C —2D 2
Hobby Clo. Chel —4F 15
Holder Rd. Bis C —3E 3
Holland Ct. Glos —6B 10
(off Denmark Rd.)
Hollis Gdns. Chel —3A 14
Hollis Rd. Chel —3A 14
Hollow La. Stro —3E 35
Holly End. Qued —5C 26
Holly Gro., The. Qued —5C 26
Hollyhock La. Pain —5H 31
Holly Tree Garden. Ebl —4F 33
Holmer Cres. Up Hat —3A 14
Holmleigh Pde. Tuf —3F 27
Holmleigh Rd. Tuf —2F 27
Holmwood Clo. Tuf —3F 27
Holmwood Dri. Tuf —3G 27
Holst Way. Tuf —3G 27
Holtham Av. C'dwn —2A 12
Holt, The. Barn —4F 21
Home Clo. Chel —4B 4
Homecroft Dri. Uck —2B 4
Home Farm Ct. Char K —2B 16
Homestead Ct. Abb —6G 21
Honeybourne Dri. Chel —3A 4
Honeybourne Rd. Chel —3A 4
Honeysuckle Clo. Pres —4D 6
Honeysuckle Dri. Abb —6E 21
Honeythorne Clo. H'std —4E 19
Honyatt Rd. Glos —6A 10
Hooper Clo. Glos —5C 20
Hope Orchard. Chel —3A 4
Hope St. Chel —4E 5
Hopewell St. Glos —3A 20
Hopwood Gro. Chel —6B 6
Hornbeam M. Longl —4C 10
Horns Rd. Stro —4E 35
Horsbere Rd. Huc —3H 21
Horsefair Clo. Char K —4B 16
Horsefair St. Char K —3B 16
Horsley Clo. Abb —6F 21
Horton Rd. Glos —2B 20
Howard Pl. Huc —4H 21
Howard St. Glos —3H 19
Howcroft. C'dwn —5B 12
Howell Rd. Chel —3B 4
(in two parts)
Howgate Clo. Abb —6G 21
Hucclecote La. C'dwn —3B 22
Hucclecote M. Huc —4G 21
Hucclecote Rd. Glos —3G 21
Hudson St. Chel —4G 5
Hulbert Clo. Swin —6A 2
Hulbert Cres. Up Hat —4C 14
Humber Pl. Brockw —6E 23
Humber Rd. Chel —5B 6
Humphreys Clo. Stro —1H 33
Hungerford St. Chel —4G 5
Hunters Clo. Stro —3G 33
Hunters Ga. A'dle —1E 29
Hunters Rd. Bis C —1D 2
Hunters Way. Stro —2G 33
Huntingdon Clo. Ebl —4G 33
Huntley Clo. Abb —6F 21
Huntscote Rd. King T —2D 4
Huntsfield Clo. Chel —3H 5
Huntsmans Clo. Bis C —1F 3
Hurcombe Way. Brockw —5D 22
Hurst Clo. Longl —4E 11
Huxley Rd. Glos —4A 20
Huxley Way. Bis C —1C 2
Hyatts Way. Bis C —2F 3
Hyde Clo. Glos —1B 20
Hyde La. Glos —1B 20
Hyde La. Pres —6C 2
Hyde Rd. Swin —1E 5
Hyett Clo. Pain —5H 31
Hyett Rd. Stro —3H 33

Icombe Clo. Bis C —2E 3
Idsall Dri. Pres —3D 6
Imjin Rd. Chel —5C 6
Imperial Cir. Chel —6G 5
Imperial La. Chel —6G 5
Imperial Sq. Chel —6G 5
India Ho. Chel —5B 4
India Rd. Glos —3B 20
(in two parts)
Innsworth La. Glos —4D 10
Innsworth Technology Pk. Inn —3D 10
Insley Gdns. Huc —3G 21
Isbourne Rd. Chel —5C 6
Ismay Rd. Chel —3B 4
Ivory Clo. Tuf —3F 27
Ivy Bank. Pres —4D 6
Ivydene. Mais —2D 8

Jackson Cres. Inn —3F 11
Jacob's Ladder. Bat —1C 16
James Donovan Ct. Chel —6B 6
James Drove. Char K —5C 16
James Grieve Rd. Abb —6G 21
James Way. Huc —5A 22
Japonica Clo. C'dwn —2H 11
Japonica Dri. Up Hat —4D 14
Jardine Dri. Bis C —1D 2
Jasmine Clo. A'dle —1E 29
Jasmin Way. Up Hat —5C 14
Javelin Way. Brockw —6E 23
Jaythorpe. A'dle —2E 29
Jenner Clo. Huc —3G 21
Jenner Gdns. Chel —5G 5
Jenner Wlk. Chel —5G 5
Jennings Wlk. Glos —2H 19
Jersey Av. Chel —5A 6
Jersey Rd. Glos —3A 20
Jersey St. Chel —5H 5
Jesson Rd. Bis C —2F 3
Jessop Av. Chel —6F 5
Jewson Clo. Tuf —3G 27
John Bevan Clo. Stro —2E 35
John Daniels Way. C'dwn —5A 12
John St. Stro —3D 34
John Wood's All. Glos —6A 10
Jordans Way. Long —3A 10
Joyner Rd. Chel —3D 4
Julian Clo. Barn —3E 21
Juniper Av. Mat —1C 28
Juniper Ct. Chel —5A 4
Juniper Way. S'hse —2C 32
Jupiter Way. Abb —5G 21
Justicia Way. Up Hat —4C 14

Katherine Clo. C'dwn —1G 11
Kaybourne Cres. Glos —4C 12
Kayte Clo. Bis C —3E 3
Kayte La. Bis C —3F 3
Keats Av. Glos —1F 27
Keats Gdns. Stro —1B 34
Keepers Mill. W'cte —2G 3
Keirle Wlk. Chel —2C 4
Kemble Clo. Tuf —3G 27
Kemble Gro. Red T —2G 13
Kemble Rd. Tuf —3H 27
Kemerton Rd. Chel —3E 15
Kempsford Acre. W'cte —2G 3
Kemps La. Pain —6H 31
Kempton Gro. Chel —5A 4
Kencourt Clo. Glos —1C 20
Kendal Rd. Glos —6D 10
Kendrick La. Stro —3D 34
Kendrick St. Stro —3D 34
Kenelm Dri. Chel —3F 15
Kenelm Gdns. Chel —3E 15
Kenilworth Av. Glos —1C 20
Kennedy Clo. Huc —2G 21
Kennel La. Brockw —1D 30
Kenneth Clo. Chel —5H 15
Kennett Gdns. Abb —1F 29
Kensington Av. Chel —1D 14
Kent Clo. C'dwn —5C 12
Kentmere Clo. Chel —2B 14
Kenton Dri. Longl —4D 10
Keriston Av. C'dwn —4H 11
Kerstin Clo. Chel —2F 5
Kestrel Clo. Chel —4F 15
Kestrel Ct. S'hse —2C 32
Kestrel Gdns. Qued —2C 26
Kestrel Pde. Inn —3E 11
(off Blackbird Av.)
Keswick Clo. Glos —6C 10
Keswick Rd. Chel —2B 14
Kevin Clo. Barn —3E 21
Kew Pl. Chel —2G 15
Kew Pl. Longl —4E 11
Keynsham Bank. Chel —1A 16
Keynshambury Rd. Chel —1H 15
Keynsham Rd. Chel —2H 15
Keynsham St. Chel —1A 16
Kidnappers La. Chel —4E 15
Kilminster Ct. C'dwn —3H 11
Kimberley Clo. Glos —5E 11
Kimberley Wlk. Chel —5C 6
Kimbrose. Glos —2H 19
Kimbrose Way. Glos —2G 19
Kimmins Rd. S'hse —2D 32
King Alfred Way. Chel —1A 16
King Arthur Clo. Chel —2A 16
King Edward's Av. Glos —5H 19
Kingfisher Rise. Qued —4A 26
King George Clo. Chel —3A 16
King Henry Clo. Chel —3A 16
Kingley Rd. Stro —3H 33
King's Barton St. Glos —2H 19
Kingsclere Dri. Bis C —2D 2
Kingscote Av. Chel —2A 14
Kingscote Clo. Chel —2A 14
Kingscote Clo. C'dwn —5C 12
Kingscote Dri. Abb —6F 21
Kingscote Gro. Chel —2A 14
Kingscote Rd. E. Chel —2A 14
Kingscote Rd. W. Chel —3A 14
Kingscourt La. Stro —5B 34
Kingscroft Rd. Huc —4G 21
Kingsditch La. Chel —3D 4
Kingsditch Retail Pk. Chel —2D 4
Kingsholm Ct. Glos —5H 9
Kingsholm Rd. Glos —6H 9
Kingsholm Sq. Glos —6H 9
Kingsley Gdns. Chel —6B 4
Kingsley Rd. Glos —6B 20
Kingsmead. Abb —1F 29
Kingsmead. Pain —5G 31
Kingsmead Av. Chel —3C 4
Kingsmead Clo. Chel —3C 4
Kingsmead Ind. Est. Chel —4D 4
Kingsmead Rd. Chel —3C 4
King's Mill La. Pain —6G 31
King's Rd. Chel —6A 6
King's Rd. S'hse —1C 32
King's Rd. Stro —4C 34
Kings Sq. Glos —1H 19
Kingston Dri. Chel —6A 4
Kingstone Av. Huc —2G 21
King St. Chel —5G 5
King St. Stro —3D 34
Kingsville Rd. King T —2D 4
Kings Wlk. Glos —2H 19
Kingswood Clo. Bis C —2E 3
King William Dri. Chel —3A 16
Kinmoor. A'dle —2E 29
Kipling Clo. Glos —1F 27
Kipling Rd. Chel —6B 4
Kitchener Av. Glos —6H 19
Kitesnest La. L'pll —6B 34
Knap La. Pain —6H 31
Knapp La. Chel —5F 5
Knapp La. Pain —1H 35
Knapp Rd. Chel —5F 5
Knapp, The. Char K —3C 16
Knightsbridge Cres. Chel —2A 16
Knoll, The. Cran —6E 31

Knoll, The. *Stro* —3E **35**
Knollys End. *Qued* —5C **26**
Knowles Rd. *Glos* —4A **20**

Laburnum Ct. *Chel* —5A **4**
Laburnum Gdns. *Qued* —4C **26**
Laburnum Rd. *Glos* —6G **19**
Laburnum Rd. *S'hse* —3B **32**
Laburnum Wlk. *S'hse* —3B **32**
Lacca Clo. *Longl* —4E **11**
Lacy Clo. *Longl* —3D **10**
Ladybellgate St. *Glos* —2G **19**
Ladychapel Rd. *Abb* —5F **21**
Ladysmith Rd. *Chel* —5C **6**
Ladysmith Rd. *Glos* —5H **19**
Ladywell Clo. *H'std* —4E **19**
Lake Ho. Pk. *Bis C* —1D **2**
Lake St. *Pres* —2C **6**
Lambert Av. *Shur* —2A **24**
Lambert Clo. *Shur* —2A **24**
Lambert Dri. *Shur* —2A **24**
Lambert Gdns. *Shur* —2A **24**
Lambert Ter. *Shur* —1A **24**
Lambourn Clo. *Longl* —6F **11**
Lampreys, The. *Glos* —5C **20**
Landor Gdns. *Chel* —5A **6**
Lanes, The. *Chel* —5E **15**
Lane, The. *Rand* —1H **33**
Langdale Gdns. *Longl* —4D **10**
Langdale Rd. *Chel* —2C **14**
Langden Rd. La. *Chel* —3G **15**
Langdon Rd. *Chel* —3G **15**
Langley Rd. *Mat* —6C **20**
Langtoft Rd. *Stro* —3F **35**
Langton Clo. *Glos* —2F **21**
Langton Gro. Rd. *Char K* —2B **16**
Langton Pl. *Char K* —2B **16**
Lanham Gdns. *Qued* —6C **26**
Lannett Rd. *Glos* —5H **19**
Lansdown. *Stro* —3D **34**
Lansdown Castle Dri. *Chel* —1C **14**
Lansdown Clo. *Chel* —1D **14**
Lansdown Ct. *Chel* —1F **15**
Lansdown Cres. *Chel* —1E **15**
Lansdown Cres. La. *Chel* —1E **15**
Lansdown Ind. Est. *Chel* —6D **4**
Lansdown Lodge Dri. *Chel* —1D **14**
Lansdown Pde. *Chel* —1E **15**
Lansdown Pl. *Chel* —1E **15**
Lansdown Pl. La. *Chel* —1E **15**
Lansdown Rd. *Chel* —1C **14**
(in two parts)
Lansdown Rd. *Glos* —6A **10**
Lansdown Ter. *Chel* —6F **5**
Lansdown Ter. La. *Chel* —6F **5**
Lansdown Wlk. *Chel* —1F **15**
Larch Clo. *Char K* —4C **16**
Larches, The. *Abb* —4F **21**
Larchmere Gro. *Up Hat* —4B **14**
Larch Rise. *Chel* —5E **15**
Larchwood Dri. *Tuf* —2H **27**
Larkham Clo. *Mat* —2C **28**
Larkham Pl. *Mat* —2C **28**
Larkhay Rd. *Huc* —3H **21**
Larksfield Rd. *K'ct* —6B **34**
Larkspear Clo. *Glos* —6H **19**
Larput Pl. *Chel* —4G **5**
Lasne Cres. *Brockw* —1E **31**
Lassington La. *H'nam* —4A **8**
(Maidenhall)
Lassington La. *H'nam* —5C **8**
(Over)
Latymer Croft. *C'dwn* —4A **12**
Laura Clo. *Longl* —5C **10**
Laurel Dri. *Pres* —3C **6**
Laurel Ga. *Abb* —1G **29**
Laurels, The. *Glos* —4A **20**
Laurence Clo. *Shur* —1A **24**
Lavender M. *Bis C* —2D **2**
Lavender Rd. *Up Hat* —4C **14**
Lavender View. *Abb* —1G **29**
Lavington Dri. *Longl* —5F **11**
Lawn Cres. *Shur* —1B **24**
Lawns, The. *A'dle* —2E **29**
Lawns, The. *S'hse* —2B **32**
Lawn, The. *Barn* —2E **21**
Lawrence Clo. *Char K* —3C **16**
Lawrence Way. *Glos* —6H **9**
Lawrence Way N. *Glos* —5G **9**
Lawson Glade. *Char K* —5B **16**
Laxton Rd. *Abb* —5H **21**
Laxton Rd. *Chel* —5B **4**
Laxton Wlk. *Chel* —5B **4**
Laynes Rd. *Huc* —4H **21**
Leacey Ct. *C'dwn* —2H **11**
Leacey M. *C'dwn* —2H **11**
Lea Cres. *Longl* —4D **10**
Leadon Clo. *Brockw* —6E **23**
Lea Rd. *Brockw* —6E **23**
Lears Dri. *Bis C* —2F **3**
Lechmere Rd. *Chel* —4B **4**
Leckhampton Farm Ct. *L'hptn* —6E **15**
Leckhampton Hill. *Ull* —4F **25**
Leckhampton La. *Shur* —1B **24**
Leckhampton Pl. *Chel* —3G **15**
Leckhampton Rd. *Chel* —3G **15**
Ledmore Rd. *Char K* —3C **16**
Lee Clo. *Chel* —4C **4**
Leighton Rd. *Chel* —6A **6**
Leinster Clo. *Chel* —3A **4**
Leonard Rd. *Glos* —5A **20**
Leven Clo. *Longl* —5E **11**
Lewis Av. *Long* —3A **10**
Lewisham Rd. *Glos* —6H **19**
Lewis Rd. *Chel* —5A **4**
Leyson Rd. *Red T* —3H **13**
Libby's Dri. *Stro* —2E **35**
Libertus Ct. *Chel* —6D **4**
Libertus Rd. *Chel* —6C **4**
Lichfield Dri. *Chel* —4D **14**
Lichfield Rd. *Glos* —3D **20**
Liddington Clo. *Chel* —5G **15**
Liddington Ind. Est. *Chel* —3G **15**
Liddington Rd. *Chel* —5G **15**
Liddington Rd. *Longl* —6F **11**
Lilac Clo. *Up Hat* —4D **14**
Lilac Way. *Qued* —4B **26**
Lilac Way. *Tuf* —2F **27**
Lilliesfield Av. *Barn* —3F **21**
Limber Hill. *Chel* —2F **5**
Lime Clo. *Pres* —2B **6**
Lime Gro. *Stro* —3D **34**
Limekiln Gro. *H'nam* —4A **8**
Limes, The. *Long* —4H **9**
Lincoln Av. *Chel* —4D **14**
Linden Av. *Pres* —2B **6**
Linden Clo. *Pres* —2B **6**
Linden Rd. *Glos* —4G **19**
Linnet Clo. *A'dle* —6D **20**
Linsley Way. *Tuf* —4G **27**
Linton Ct. *Chel* —2H **15**
Linwell Clo. *Chel* —2E **5**
Linworth Rd. *Bis C* —2F **3**
Lion Clo. *Qued* —3C **26**
Lipson Rd. *Chel* —3B **4**
Lit. Acorns. *Bis C* —1D **2**
Lit. Bayshill M. *Chel* —6G **5**
Lit. Bayshill Ter. *Chel* —6F **5**
Lit. Cheyne. *S'hse* —2B **32**
Lit. Cleevemount. *Chel* —4A **6**
Littlecote Clo. *Bis C* —2D **2**
Littledown Rd. *Chel* —5H **15**
Lit. Elmbridge. *Longl* —5F **11**
Littlefield Clo. *Qued* —3B **26**
Lit. Herbert's Clo. *Char K* —4C **16**
Lit. Herbert's Rd. *Char K* —4C **16**
Lit. Lancarridge. *H'nam* —4A **8**
Lit. Normans. *Longl* —4D **10**
Lit. Orchard. *Bis C* —1D **2**
Lit. Pheasants. *Char K* —4B **16**
Little Wlk. *Longl* —4D **10**
Llandilo St. *Glos* —4A **20**
Llanthony Rd. *H'std* —2F **19**
Lloyd Baker Ct. *Hard* —6B **26**
Lobleys Dri. *Abb* —6G **21**
Locking Hill. *Stro* —3D **34**
Lodgemore Clo. *Stro* —3B **34**
Lodgemore La. *Stro* —3B **34**
London Rd. *Chel* —1A **16**
London Rd. *Glos* —1A **20**
London Rd. *Stro* —4D **34**
Longborough Dri. *Abb* —6F **21**
Long Field. *H'nam* —4A **8**
Longfield. *Qued* —3B **26**
Longford La. *Long* —3A **10**
Longford M. *Long* —3A **10**
Longhope Clo. *Abb* —6F **21**
Longland Ct. *Glos* —5C **10**
Longland Gdns. *Glos* —5C **10**
Longlands Clo. *Bis C* —1G **3**
Longlands Rd. *Bis C* —2F **3**
Longleat Av. *Tuf* —4F **27**
Longleat Ho. *Char K* —4B **16**
Long Mynd Av. *Up Hat* —3B **14**
Longney Rd. *Tuf* —2G **27**
Longsmith St. *Glos* —1G **19**
Longville Clo. *Abb* —6G **21**
Longway Av. *Char K* —5A **16**
Lonsdale Rd. *Glos* —1D **20**
Lords Grn. *W'cte* —2H **3**
Loriners Clo. *Qued* —3C **26**
Lovage Clo. *C'dwn* —3G **11**
Lovedays Mead. *Stro* —2D **34**
Lwr. Churchfield Rd. *Stro* —4E **35**
Lwr. Leazes. *Stro* —3E **35**
Lwr. Meadow. *Qued* —6C **26**
Lwr. Mill St. *Chel* —5E **5**
Lwr. Quay St. *Glos* —1G **19**
Lwr. Spillman's. *Stro* —4B **34**
Lower St. *Stro* —4E **35**
Lwr. Tuffley La. *Glos* —1E **27**
Lwr. Washwell La. *Pain* —5H **31**
Loweswater Clo. *Chel* —2C **14**
Loweswater Rd. *Chel* —2C **14**
Luke La. *Inn* —3F **11**
Luke Rd. *Inn* —3F **11**
Lyefield Clo. *Char K* —3B **16**
Lyefield Rd. E. *Char K* —3B **16**
Lyefield Rd. W. *Char K* —3B **16**
Lygon Wlk. *Chel* —4C **4**
Lyndhurst Vale. *W'cte* —2G **3**
Lyndley Chase. *Bis C* —2C **2**
Lyng Clo. *Barn* —3F **21**
Lynmouth Rd. *Huc* —5G **21**
Lynton Rd. *Huc* —4G **21**
Lynworth Ct. *Chel* —4B **6**
Lynworth Exchange. *Chel* —4B **6**
Lynworth Pl. *Chel* —4B **6**
Lypiatt Dri. *Chel* —1F **15**
Lypiatt La. *Chel* —1F **15**
Lypiatt M. *Chel* —1F **15**
Lypiatt Rd. *Chel* —1F **15**
Lypiatt St. *Chel* —2F **15**
Lypiatt Ter. *Chel* —1F **15**
Lysander Ct. *C'dwn* —4B **12**
Lyson's Av. *Glos* —4G **19**

Mackenzie Way. *Swin* —2D **4**
Madleaze Rd. *Glos* —3F **19**
Madleaze Trad. Est. *Glos* —3F **19**
Magdala Rd. *Glos* —2B **20**
Magnolia Ct. *Chel* —5A **4**
Magnolia Wlk. *Qued* —4B **26**
Magpie Ct. *S'hse* —2C **32**
Maida Vale Rd. *Chel* —3G **15**
Maidenhall. *H'nam* —4A **8**
Mainard Sq. *Longl* —4D **10**
Main Rd. *Shur* —2A **24**
Maisemore Rd. *Mais* —3E **9**
Malden Rd. *Chel* —5H **5**
Maldon Gdns. *Glos* —4A **20**
Malet Clo. *Longl* —4D **10**
Mallard Clo. *Qued* —4A **26**
Malmesbury Rd. *Glos* —4C **20**
Malmesbury Rd. *King T* —2D **4**
Malthouse La. *Chel* —4G **5**
Malvern Gdns. *Stro* —3H **33**
Malvern Pl. *Chel* —6F **5**
Malvern Rd. *Chel* —6E **5**
Malvern Rd. *Glos* —5A **10**
Malverns, The. *A'dle* —5E **21**
Malvern St. *Chel* —3E **5**
Malvern View Bus. Pk. *Bis C* —1C **2**
Manchester Pk. *Chel* —3D **4**
Manchester Way. *Chel* —4F **5**
Mandara Gro. *A'dle* —1E **29**
Mandarin Way. *Chel* —2E **5**
Mandeville Clo. *Longl* —4D **10**
Mankley Rd. *Leon S* —6C **32**
Manley Gdns. *Longl* —4D **10**
Manor Ct. *Swin* —1D **4**
Manor Gdns. *Glos* —3F **21**
Manor Pk. *Longl* —5F **11**
Manor Pk. *Up Hat* —4A **14**
Manor Rd. *Swin* —2C **4**
Manor, The. *C'dwn* —5B **12**
Manor View. *Sel E* —6H **33**
Manse Gdns. *Chel* —2C **14**
Mansell Clo. *Pod* —6F **19**
Manser St. *Chel* —4G **5**
Mansfield M. *Qued* —6C **26**
Maple Clo. *Hard* —5A **26**
Maple Dri. *Brockw* —4C **22**
Maple Dri. *Char K* —4C **16**
Maple Dri. *Stro* —1B **34**
Maples, The. *Abb* —4F **21**
Marchant Clo. *Chel* —4C **4**
Marefield Clo. *Barn* —4F **21**
Margrett Rd. *Chel* —4G **5**
Marian Ct. *Glos* —1G **19**
Marjoram Clo. *Abb* —6G **21**
Market Pde. *Glos* —1H **19**
Market St. *Chel* —5F **5**
Market Way. *Glos* —2H **19**
Marlborough Clo. *Bis C* —2D **2**
Marlborough Clo. *Chel* —2A **16**
Marlborough Cres. *Glos* —4B **20**
Marlborough Rd. *Glos* —4B **20**
Marle Hill Pde. *Chel* —4G **5**
Marle Hill Rd. *Chel* —4G **5**
Marleyfield Clo. *C'dwn* —2H **11**
Marleyfield Way. *C'dwn* —2H **11**
Marling Cres. *Stro* —3A **34**
Marram Clo. *Abb* —6G **21**
Marsh Clo. *Chel* —4F **5**
Marsh Dri. *Chel* —3F **5**
Marsh Gdns. *Chel* —4F **5**
Marsh La. *Chel* —4F **5**
Marsh Rd. *Leon S* —6B **32**
Marsh Ter. *Shur* —1A **24**
Marsland Rd. *Chel* —5A **4**
Marston Rd. *Chel* —3A **6**
Marten Clo. *Abb* —6H **21**
Martindale Rd. *C'dwn* —3A **12**
Martins, The. *Stro* —2G **33**
Mary Gro. *H'nam* —4A **8**
Mary Rose Av. *C'dwn* —2G **11**
Masefield Av. *Glos* —1F **27**
Mason Rd. *Stro* —3G **35**
Massey Pde. *Glos* —4A **20**
Massey Rd. *Glos* —4B **20**
Maston Pl. *Glos* —4B **20**
Mathews Way. *Stro* —2A **34**
Matson Av. *Mat* —1D **28**
Matson La. *Mat* —1C **28**
Matson Pl. *Glos* —4B **20**
Maverdine Ct. Glos —1G ***19***
(off Clare St.)
Mayall Ct. *Mat* —2D **28**
Mayfair Clo. *H'std* —3F **19**
Mayfield Clo. *Bis C* —3E **3**
Mayfield Dri. *Huc* —3G **21**
Maythorn Dri. *Chel* —3A **4**
May Tree Sq. *Glos* —4D **20**
Mead Clo. *Chel* —4H **15**
Meade-King Gro. *W'cte* —2G **3**
Meadoway. *Bis C* —3D **2**
Meadow Clo. *Chel* —1H **13**
Meadowcroft. *Abb* —6F **21**
Meadow La. *Dud* —4H **33**
Meadow La. *Up Hat* —4B **14**
Meadow Lea. *Bis C* —3D **2**
Meadowleaze. *Glos* —6E **11**
Meadow Rd. *S'hse* —2C **32**
Meadow Way. *C'dwn* —2A **12**
Mead Rd. *Abb* —6F **21**
Mead Rd. *Chel* —3G **15**
Mead Rd. Trad. Est. Chel —3G ***15***
(off Mead Rd.)
Meads Clo. *Bis C* —2F **3**
Meadvale Clo. *Long* —3A **10**
Meadway Rd. *S'hse* —4B **32**
Medoc Clo. *Chel* —2E **5**
Medway Cres. *Brockw* —6E **23**
Meerstone Way. *A'dle* —2E **29**
Melbourne Clo. *Chel* —3F **15**
Melbourne Clo. *S'hse* —1C **32**
Melbourne Dri. *S'hse* —1B **32**
Melbourne St. E. *Glos* —4A **20**
Melbourne St. W. *Glos* —4A **20**
Meldon Ter. *Stro* —3C **34**
Melick Clo. *Glos* —6B **20**
Melody Way. *Longl* —4F **11**
Melville Rd. *C'dwn* —4A **12**
Mendip Clo. *Chel* —4B **6**
Mendip Clo. *Qued* —5B **26**
Mendip Rd. *Chel* —4B **6**
Merchants Mead. *Qued* —4A **26**
Merchants Quay. *Doc T* —2G **19**
Merchant's Rd. *Glos* —3G **19**
Mercian Ct. *Chel* —2F **15**
Mercia Rd. *Glos* —6H **9**
Mercury Way. *Abb* —5G **21**
Meredith Cotts. *Glos* —4C **20**
Merestones Clo. *Chel* —3E **15**
Merestones Dri. *Chel* —3E **15**
Merestones Rd. *Chel* —3E **15**
Merevale Rd. *Glos* —6C **10**
Merlin Clo. *Chel* —4F **15**
Merlin Dri. *Qued* —3B **26**
Merlin Way. *Chel* —4F **15**
Merriville Gdns. *Chel* —4D **4**
Merriville Rd. *Chel* —4D **4**
Merrywalks. *Stro* —3C **34**
Merrywalks Shopping Cen. Stro
(off Merrywalks) —3D ***34***
Mersey Rd. *Chel* —5B **6**
Merton Clo. *S'hse* —4E **33**
Meteor Way. *Brockw* —6D **22**
Metz Way. *Glos* —2A **20**
Michaelmas Ct. *Glos* —6B **10**
Mickle Mead. H'nam —4A ***8***
(off Poole Ground)
Middlehay Ct. *Bis C* —2D **2**
Middle Hill. *Stro* —3E **35**
Middle Leazes. *Stro* —3E **35**

Middle Spillman's. Stro —4B 34
Middle St. Stro —3D 34
Middle St. Upl —2D 34
Middleton Lawn. Inn —3F 11
Midland Rd. Glos —3H 19
Midland Rd. S'hse —2B 32
Midwinter Av. Chel —4F 5
Midwinter Gdns. Chel —3F 5
Milford Clo. Glos —4C 10
Millbridge Rd. Huc —4H 21
Millbrook Clo. Glos —2B 20
Millbrook Gdns. Chel —5E 5
Millbrook St. Chel —5E 5
Millbrook St. Glos —3A 20
Miller Clo. Longl —4E 11
Millers Dyke. Qued —4A 26
Millers Grn. Glos —1H 19
Mill Farm Dri. Stro —2H 33
Millfields. Huc —3H 21
Mill Gro. Qued —4A 26
Millham Rd. Bis C —1F 3
Mill Ho. Dri. Chel —2F 5
Millin Av. Tuf —2G 27
Mill La. Brockw —5D 22
Mill La. Char K —6E 7
Mill La. Pres —3D 6
Mill La. Wit —1F 31
Mill St. Glos —2B 20
Mill St. Pres —2C 6
Milne Wlk. Chel —3B 4
Milo Pl. Glos —5H 19
Milsom St. Chel —5G 5
Milton Av. Chel —1C 14
Milton Av. Glos —6F 19
Milton Gro. Stro —3F 35
Milton Rd. Chel —6B 4
Mimosa Av. Up Hat —5D 14
Mimosa Ct. C'dwn —2H 11
Minerva Clo. Abb —5G 21
Minetts Av. Bis C —2F 3
Minster Clo. Bis C —1D 2
Minster Gdns. Abb —5G 21
Minstrel Way. C'dwn —1G 11
Miserden Rd. Chel —1A 14
Mistletoe M. C'dwn —3G 11
Mitre St. Chel —1H 15
Moat La. Uck —1A 4
Moat, The. Qued —4C 26
Mogridge Clo. Glos —4H 21
Monarch Clo. Abb —1F 29
Monica Dri. Chel —3H 5
Monkey Puzzle Clo. Ebl —4A 34
Monk Meadow Rd. H'std —3F 19
Monkmeadow Trad. Est. H'std —4F 19
Monks Croft. Chel —6B 4
Monson Av. Chel —5G 5
Montfort Rd. Glos —4C 10
Montgomery Rd. Chel —3A 14
Montpelier. Glos —2H 19
Montpellier Arc. Chel —1G 15
(off Monpellier Av.)
Montpellier Av. Chel —1G 15
Montpellier Ct. Chel —1F 15
Montpellier Dri. Chel —1G 15
Montpellier Exchange. Chel —1F 15
(off Montpellier St.)
Montpellier Gro. Chel —2G 15
Montpellier Ho. Chel —1F 15
Montpellier M. Glos —2H 19
Montpellier Pde. Chel —1G 15
Montpellier Retreat. Chel —2G 15
Montpellier Spa Rd. Chel —1G 15
Montpellier St. Chel —1F 15
Montpellier Ter. Chel —1F 15
Montpellier Vs. Chel —2G 15
Montpellier Wlk. Chel —1F 15
Montreal Ho. Chel —4B 4
Moor Court Dri. Chel —5A 6
Moorend Cres. Chel —3F 15
Moorend Glade. Char K —3A 16
Moorend Gro. Chel —4F 15
Moorend Pk. Rd. Chel —3F 15
Moorend Rd. Char K —4A 16
Moorend Rd. Chel —4G 15
Moorend St. Chel —3F 15
Moorfield Rd. Brockw —5D 22
Moor Hall Pl. Stro —2H 33
Moorhen Ct. Qued —4A 26
Moorlands Trad. Est. Glos —3G 19
Moors Av. Chel —3D 4
Moor St. Glos —4B 20
Moreton Clo. Bis C —3F 3
Moreton St. Glos —4A 20
Moreton Ter. Char K —2B 16
Morlands Dri. Char K —5C 16
Morley Av. C'dwn —3H 11
Morningside. Pres —3D 6
Morningside Clo. Pres —3D 6
Morningside Courtyard. Pres —3D 6
Mornington Dri. Chel —3G 15
Morpeth St. Glos —4A 20
Morris Ct. Chel —2C 14
Morris Hill Clo. Swin —1E 5
Mortimer Rd. Longl —4D 10
Morton Cotts. Glos —2A 20
Morwent Clo. Abb —5F 21
Moselle Dri. C'dwn —3H 11
Mosley Cres. Stro —3H 33
Mosley Rd. Stro —2H 33
Mostham Pl. Brockw —5C 22
Mottershead Dri. Inn —2F 11
Mount St. Glos —1G 19
Mowberry Clo. Longl —4D 10
Mulberry Clo. Hard —5B 26
Mulberry Ct. Chel —5A 4
Munsley Gro. Mat —2D 28
Murray Clo. Bis C —1E 3
Murvagh Clo. Chel —2H 15
Muscroft Rd. Pres —3E 7
Mutsilver M. Longl —4F 11
Myers Rd. Glos —2B 20
Myrtle Clo. Glos —6B 20

Naas La. Qued —6C 26
Nailsworth Ter. Chel —5F 5
(off Hereford Pl.)
Napier St. Glos —2A 20
Naseby Ho. Chel —4B 6
Natton Cotts. Char K —2E 17
Naunton Cres. Chel —3G 15
Naunton La. Chel —3G 15
Naunton Pde. Chel —2G 15
Naunton Pk. Clo. Chel —3H 15
Naunton Pk. Rd. Chel —3H 15
Naunton Rd. Glos —4E 21
Naunton Ter. Chel —2G 15
Naunton Way. Chel —3G 15
Needham Av. Qued —6E 27
Nelmes Row. Char K —4D 16
Nelson St. Glos —5A 20
Nelson St. Stro —3D 34
Nene Clo. Qued —3B 26
Neptune Clo. Abb —5G 21
Netheridge Clo. H'std —1D 26
Netherwood Clo. Chel —4D 4
Netherwood Gdns. Chel —4D 4
Nettleton Rd. Chel —2A 14
Nettleton Rd. Glos —2A 20
Newark Ho. H'std —4E 19
Newark Rd. Glos —5F 19
New Barn Av. Chel —3B 6
New Barn Clo. Chel —3B 6
New Barn La. Chel —2H 5
New Barn M. Chel —3C 6
Newcourt Pk. Char K —3B 16
Newcourt Rd. Char K —3A 16
Newent Rd. H'nam —4A 8
New Inn La. Glos —1H 19
Newland St. Glos —1A 20
New Rd. Sel —5H 33
New Rd. W'cte —3H 3
New Rutland Ct. Chel —5G 5
Newstead Rd. Barn —3F 21
New St. Char K —4B 16
New St. Chel —5F 5
New St. Glos —3G 19
New St. K Stan —6D 32
New St. Pain —5H 31
Newton Av. Glos —4D 20
Newton Clo. Chel —5B 4
Newton Rd. Chel —5B 4
Newton's Way. Stro —4C 34
New Zealand Ho. Chel —4C 4
Nickleby Bungalows. Glos —6A 20
Nicolson Clo. Glos —2F 11
Nightingale Croft. Inn —3E 11
Nine Elms Rd. Longl —5F 11
Noake Rd. Huc —3H 21
Norbury Av. Mat —6C 20
Norfolk Av. Chel —6C 4
Norfolk St. Glos —2G 19
Normal Ter. Chel —5G 5
Norman Bill Way. Glos —2C 20
Nortenham Clo. Bis C —1C 2
Northbank Clo. Red T —2G 13
Northbrook Rd. Glos —2D 20
Northfield M. Stro —2D 34
Northfield Pas. Chel —5H 5
Northfield Rd. Glos —6A 20
Northfield Sq. Glos —6A 20
Northfield Ter. Chel —5H 5
Northgate St. Glos —1H 19
N. Hall M. Chel —5A 6
North Pl. Chel —5H 5
North Rd. Glos —5A 10
North Rd. E. Red T —2G 13
North Rd. W. Red T —2F 13
North St. Chel —5G 5
N. Upton La. Barn —4F 21
Norwich Dri. Chel —3D 14
Norwood Rd. Chel —2G 15
Notgrove Clo. Chel —1B 14
Notgrove Clo. Tuf —3F 27
Notley Pl. Huc —4H 21
Nottingham Rd. Bis C —1E 3
Nouncells Cross. Stro —3E 35
Nourse Clo. Chel —5E 15
Noverton Av. Pres —3E 7
Noverton La. Pres —3D 6
Nunney Clo. Chel —1H 13
Nurseries, The. Bis C —3D 2
Nursery Clo. Stro —4E 35
Nursery Ter. S'hse —4C 32
Nursery, The. K Stan —6D 32
Nut Hill. Upton L —5H 29
Nutley Av. Tuf —3F 27
Nutmeg Clo. A'dle —1E 29
Nympsfield Rd. Tuf —2G 27

Oak Av. Char K —2B 16
Oakbank. Glos —1H 27
Oakbrook Dri. Red T —2H 13
Oak Cotts. Upton L —3F 29
Oakcroft Clo. Mat —2E 29
Oakdene. Chel —1E 15
Oak Dri. Brockw —5C 22
Oak Dri. Rod —4C 34
Oakfield Rd. Bis C —2F 3
Oakfield St. Chel —2E 15
Oakhurst Clo. C'dwn —4H 11
Oakhurst Rise. Chel —1B 16
Oakland Av. Chel —3A 6
Oakland St. Char K —2B 16
Oakleaze. Glos —6E 11
Oakley Rd. Bat —1B 16
Oak Mnr. Dri. Chel —6B 6
Oakridge. H'nam —4A 8
Oakridge Clo. Abb —6F 21
Oaks, The. Abb —4F 21
Oaks, The. Up Hat —3A 14
Oak Tree Clo. Hard —6B 26
Oaktree Gdns. Mat —2D 28
Oak Way. S'hse —3C 32
Oakwood Dri. Huc —5G 21
Oatfield. Qued —3B 26
O'Brien Rd. Chel —3D 4
Ogbourne Clo. Longl —6F 11
Okus Rd. Char K —4B 16
Old Acre Dri. Bis C —1F 3
Old Bath Rd. Chel —6G 15
Oldbury Clo. Chel —4B 4
Oldbury Orchard. C'dwn —5C 12
Oldbury Rd. Chel —4B 4
Old Cheltenham Rd. Longl —5E 11
Oldends La. S'hse —3A 32
Oldfield Cres. Chel —1C 14
Old Gloucester Rd. H'den —2A 4
Old Millbrook Ter. Chel —5E 5
Old Painswick Clo. Glos —5C 20
Old Painswick Rd. Glos —5C 20
Old Rectory Pl. Stro —5B 34
Old Reddings Clo. Red T —2H 13
Old Reddings Rd. Red T —2H 13
Old Rd. Mais —1D 8
Old Rd. Sthm —5H 3
Old Row. Glos —3A 20
Old School M., The. Char K —3C 16
Old Station Dri. Chel —3G 15
Old Tewkesbury Rd. Nor —4A 10
Old Tram Rd. Glos —2G 19
Oldway. Upton L —3F 29
Olio La. Chel —1G 15
(in two parts)
Oliver Clo. Tuf —3G 27
Olympus Pk. Ind. Est. Qued —3D 26
Orangery, The. Barn —4F 21
Orchard Av. Chel —4B 4
Orchard Cvn. Pk. Huc —5H 21
Orchard Clo. Hard —6A 26
Orchard Clo. Leon S —6C 32
Orchard Clo. Long —4H 9
Orchard Cotts. Char K —2E 17
Orchard Ct. Pain —6H 31
Orchard Ct. S'hse —3B 32
Orchard Dri. C'dwn —5C 12
Orchard Gro., The. Shur —2A 24
Orchard Ho. Bis C —2E 3
Orchard Mead. Pain —6H 31
Orchard Pk. Chel —2C 4
Orchard Pl. Chel —5G 5
Orchard Pl. S'hse —3B 32
Orchard Rd. Bis C —2E 3
Orchard Rd. Ebl —4F 33
Orchard Rd. Longl —5F 11
Orchards, The. Huc —5H 21
Orchard View. L'pll —6B 34
Orchard Way. Chel —4C 4
Orchard Way. C'dwn —2A 12
Orchard Way. Mais —2D 8
Organ's All. Glos —2H 19
Oriel Rd. Chel —6G 5
Oriel School Dri. Sthm —6H 3
Oriel Ter. Chel —6G 5
Oriole Way. A'dle —5D 20
Ormond Pl. Chel —6G 5
Ormond Ter. Chel —6G 5
Orrisdale Ter. Chel —1H 15
Osborne Av. Tuf —4F 27
Osier Clo. Glos —1B 28
Osprey Clo. A'dle —6E 21
Osprey Dri. S'hse —2C 32
Osprey Rd. Chel —4F 15
Osric Rd. Glos —5A 20
Otter Rd. Abb —6H 21
Oval, The. Glos —5G 19
Overbrook Clo. Glos —2D 20
Overbrook Dri. Chel —4A 6
Overbrook Rd. Hard —5B 26
Overbury Rd. Glos —3B 20
Overbury St. Char K —2B 16
Over Causeway. Glos —6D 8
Overton Ct. Chel —6F 5
Overton Pk. Rd. Chel —6F 5
Overton Rd. Chel —6F 5
Owl Clo. A'dle —6E 21
Owls End Rd. Bis C —1F 3
Oxbutts Pk. W'cte —1G 3
Oxebode, The. Glos —1H 19
Oxford Clo. Chel —1A 16
Oxford Pde. Chel —1H 15
Oxford Pas. Chel —5G 5
Oxford Rd. Glos —6A 10
Oxford St. Chel —1A 16
Oxford St. Glos —1A 20
Oxford Ter. Glos —1A 20
Oxford Ter. Upl —2D 34
(off Middle St.)
Oxford Way. Chel —4D 14
Oxmead Clo. Bis C —1G 3
Oxmoor. A'dle —2E 29
Oxstalls Dri. Longl —4B 10
Oxstalls La. Longl —6C 10
Oxstalls Way. Longl —5C 10

Paddock Gdns. Longl —4E 11
Paddock Rise. S'hse —3C 32
Paddocks La. Chel —3G 5
Paddocks, The. H'std —5E 19
Paganhill Est. Stro —2A 34
Paganhill La. Stro —3A 34
Pagets Rd. Bis C —3F 3
Painswick Old Rd. Stro —2C 34
Painswick Rd. Chel —3F 15
Painswick Rd. Cran & Brockw —6B 30
Painswick Rd. Mat —4B 20
Painswick Rd. Stro —1C 34
Pakistan Ho. Chel —5B 4
Palmer Av. Abb —6G 21
Parabola Clo. Chel —6F 5
Parabola La. Chel —6F 5
Parabola Rd. Chel —6F 5
Parade, The. Brockw —5F 11
Paragon Ter. Chel —1G 15
Park Av. Longl —4D 10
Park Brake. H'nam —5A 8
Parkbury Clo. Chel —5D 4
Park Ct. Stro —4E 35
Park Dri. Qued —4C 26
Parkend Rd. Glos —4H 19
Park Ga. Chel —2F 15
Park Ho. Chel —2F 15
Parkland Rd. Chel —5A 16
Parklands. C'dwn —3G 11
Parklands. Qued —4C 26
Park La. Pres —1C 6
Park M. Chel —3F 15
Park Pde. S'hse —2B 32
Park Pl. Chel —2F 15
Park Rd. Glos —2H 19
Park Rd. S'hse —3B 32
Park Rd. Stro —4E 35
Parkside Clo. C'dwn —3G 11
Parkside Dri. C'dwn —3G 11
Park St. Chel —5F 5
Park St. Glos —1H 19

Park, The. *Chel* —2F **15**
Park View Dri. *Stro* —2H **33**
Parkwood Cres. *Huc* —5G **21**
Parkwood Gro. *Char K* —5B **16**
Parliament Clo. *Stro* —3D **34**
Parliament St. *Glos* —2H **19**
Parliament St. *Stro* —3D **34**
Parr Clo. *C'dwn* —2G **11**
Parrish Cres. *A'dle* —1E **29**
Parry Rd. *Glos* —5A **20**
Parton Dri. *C'dwn* —4B **12**
Parton M. *C'dwn* —3A **12**
Parton Rd. *C'dwn* —2H **11**
Partridge Clo. *Pod* —6F **19**
Partridge Clo. *S'hse* —2C **32**
Pate Ct. *Chel* —5G **5**
Pates Av. *Chel* —5E **5**
Patseamur M. *Inn* —4F **11**
Patterdale Clo. *Chel* —2C **4**
Paul St. *Glos* —4A **20**
Paygrove La. *Longl* —5E **11**
Paynes Pitch. *C'dwn* —5C **12**
Paynes Pl. *Stro* —4A **34**
Peacock Clo. *Abb* —6F **21**
Peacock Clo. *Chel* —5A **4**
Peakstile Piece. *W'cte* —2G **3**
Pearce Way. *Glos* —1E **27**
Pearcroft Rd. *S'hse* —3C **32**
Peart Clo. *Glos* —2B **20**
Pear Tree Clo. *Hard* —6B **26**
Pear Tree Clo. *W'cte* —2H **3**
Pearwood Way. *Tuf* —3F **27**
Pecked La. *Bis C* —1F **3**
Peel Cen., The. *Glos* —3G **19**
Peel Clo. *Char K* —4D **16**
Pegasus Gdns. *Qued* —3C **26**
Peggoty Bungalows. Glos —4D **20**
(off Stanway Rd.)
Peghouse Clo. *Stro* —1E **35**
Peghouse Rise. *Stro* —1E **35**
Pelham Cres. *C'dwn* —3H **11**
Pembridge Clo. *Char K* —3D **16**
Pembroke Rd. *Chel* —3B **14**
Pembroke St. *Glos* —3A **20**
Pembury Rd. *Glos* —1H **27**
Pendil Clo. *Chel* —1E **5**
Pendock Clo. *Qued* —4B **26**
Penharva Clo. *Chel* —4D **4**
Penhill Rd. *Mat* —1C **28**
Pennine Clo. *Qued* —5B **26**
Pennine Rd. *Chel* —3C **6**
Pennsylvania Av. *Chel* —4C **4**
Penny Clo. *Longl* —5E **11**
Penrith Rd. *Chel* —2C **14**
Penrose Rd. *Inn* —3E **11**
Pentathlon Way. *Chel* —2G **5**
Percy St. *Glos* —4A **20**
Peregrine Rd. *Chel* —4F **15**
Peregrine Way. *Qued* —2C **26**
Perry Orchard. *Stro* —2G **33**
Perry Orchard. *Upton L* —3F **29**
Persh La. *Mais* —2C **8**
Persh Way. *Mais* —2D **8**
Perth. *S'hse* —1B **32**
Peter Pennell Clo. *Chel* —3A **4**
Peters Field. *H'nam* —4B **8**
Petworth Clo. *Tuf* —5F **27**
Pheasant La. *Chel* —1G **13**
Pheasant Mead. *S'hse* —2C **32**
Philip St. *Glos* —4G **19**
Piccadilly. *Stro* —3E **35**
Piccadilly Way. *Pres* —3E **7**
Pickering Clo. *Chel* —3F **15**
Pickering Rd. *Chel* —3F **15**
Pickwick Clo. *Glos* —6E **11**
Piece, The. *C'dwn* —5C **12**
Piggy La. *Tuf* —3H **27**
Pilford Av. *Chel* —5H **15**
Pilford Clo. *Chel* —5H **15**
Pilford Ct. *Chel* —6H **15**
Pilford Rd. *Chel* —6H **15**
Pilgrim Clo. *Abb* —5F **21**
Pilgrove Clo. *Chel* —2A **4**
Pilgrove Way. *Chel* —2A **4**
Pillcroft Clo. *Wit* —1F **31**
Pillcroft Rd. *Wit* —1F **31**
Pilley Cres. *Chel* —5G **15**
Pilley La. *Chel* —5G **15**
Pincoate. *H'nam* —4A **8**
Pine Bank. *Bis C* —2G **3**
Pine Clo. *Char K* —1B **16**
Pinemount Rd. *Huc* —4H **21**
Pinery Rd. *Barn* —4F **21**
Pine Tree Dri. *Barn* —3F **21**
Pineway. *A'dle* —5C **20**
Pinewood Rd. *Glos* —5B **26**
Pinlocks. *Upton L* —2F **29**
Pipers Gro. *H'nam* —4A **8**
Pippin Clo. *Abb* —5H **21**
Pirton Cres. *C'dwn* —4A **12**
Pirton La. *C'dwn* —3H **11**
Pirton Meadow. *C'dwn* —4H **11**
Pitman Rd. *Chel* —6B **4**
Pitt Mill Gdns. *Huc* —3H **21**
Pitt St. *Glos* —1H **19**
Pittville Cir. *Chel* —5A **6**
Pittville Cir. Rd. *Chel* —5A **6**
Pittville Ct. *Chel* —3A **6**
Pittville Cres. *Chel* —4A **6**
Pittville Cres. La. *Chel* —4A **6**
Pittville Lawn. *Chel* —5H **5**
Pittville M. *Chel* —5H **5**
Pittville St. *Chel* —6H **5**
Plain, The. *W'hll* —1B **34**
Plock Ct. *Long* —4A **10**
Plocks, The. *C'dwn* —4C **12**
Plum Tree Clo. *Abb* —1F **29**
Podsmead Ct. *Glos* —1G **27**
Podsmead Pl. *Glos* —6G **19**
Podsmead Rd. *Glos* —1F **27**
Polefield Gdns. *Chel* —1E **15**
Poole Ground. *H'nam* —4A **8**
Pooles La. *Sel* —5H **33**
Poole Way. *Chel* —5F **5**
Popes Clo. *Chel* —4G **5**
Popes Meade. *H'nam* —4A **8**
Poplar Clo. *Glos* —6G **19**
Poplar Dri. *W'cte* —2H **3**
Poplars, The. *Up Hat* —4B **14**
Poplar Way. *Hard* —6B **26**
Poppy Field. *H'nam* —4B **8**
Porchester Rd. *Huc* —3G **21**
Portland Pl. *Chel* —5H **5**
Portland Sq. *Chel* —5H **5**
Portland St. *Chel* —5H **5**
Porturet Way. *Char K* —3C **16**
Portway. *Upton L* —4G **29**
Postlip Way. *Chel* —1A **14**
Post Office La. *Chel* —6G **5**
Posy La. *Glos* —6B **10**
Potters Field Rd. *W'cte* —2H **3**
Pound Clo. *Brockw* —1D **30**
Poxon Ct. *Stro* —5B **34**
Prescott Av. *Mat* —1C **28**
Prescott Wlk. *Chel* —3C **6**
Prestbury Grn. Dri. *Pres* —3D **6**
Prestbury Rd. *Chel* —5H **5**
Price St. *Glos* —4G **19**
Primrose Clo. *Glos* —1B **28**
Prince Albert Ct. *Huc* —5B **22**
Prince's Rd. *Chel* —2E **15**
Princes Rd. *Stro* —2H **33**
Princess Elizabeth Way. *Chel* —6A **4**
(in two parts)
Prince's St. *Chel* —6A **6**
Prince St. *Glos* —2A **20**
Prinknash Clo. *Mat* —1D **28**
Prinknash Rd. *Mat* —1D **28**
(in two parts)
Print Box La. *Chel* —2F **15**
Priors Rd. *Char K* —6B **6**
Priory La. *Bis C* —1F **3**
Priory Pl. *Chel* —1H **15**
Priory Pl. *Glos* —2H **19**
Priory Rd. *Glos* —1G **19**
(Clare St.)
Priory Rd. *Glos* —6H **9**
(St. Oswald's Rd.)
Priory St. *Chel* —1H **15**
Priory Ter. *Chel* —6A **6**
Priory Wlk. *Chel* —6A **6**
Promenade. *Chel* —6G **5**
Promenade, The. *Glos* —2H **19**
Providence Sq. *Chel* —5A **6**
Pullar Clo. *Bis C* —1E **3**
Pullar Ct. *Bis C* —1E **3**
Pullens Rd. *Pain* —4H **31**
Pullman Ct. *Glos* —1A **20**
Pumphrey's Rd. *Char K* —4B **16**
Purbeck Way. *Pres* —4D **6**
Purcell Rd. *C'dwn* —1G **11**
Purs La. Clo. *Glos* —1C **28**
Pyrton M. *Up Hat* —4B **14**

Quail Clo. *Barn* —4F **21**
Quantock Rd. *Qued* —5B **26**
Quat Goose La. *Swin* —6A **2**
Quay St. *Glos* —1G **19**
Quay, The. *Glos* —1G **19**
Quebec Ho. *Chel* —4B **4**
Quedgeley Pk. *Glos* —2D **26**
Queen's Cir. *Chel* —6G **5**
Queens Clo. *Huc* —2H **21**
Queen's Ct. *Chel* —1D **14**
Queen's Dri. *Stro* —2H **33**
Queens La. *Chel* —1F **15**
Queensmead. *Pain* —6G **31**
Queens Pde. *Chel* —1F **15**
Queen's Retreat. *Chel* —5E **5**
Queen's Rd. *Chel* —6D **4**
Queen's Rd. *S'hse* —3C **32**
Queen's Rd. *Stro* —4C **34**
Queens Sq. *Stro* —3E **35**
Queen St. *Chel* —4F **5**
Queens Wlk. *Glos* —2H **19**
Queenwood Gro. *Pres* —2E **7**
Quenney's Clo. *Mat* —2D **28**
Quietways. *S'hse* —2B **32**
Quinton Clo. *C'dwn* —3A **12**

Radnor Rd. *Chel* —3B **14**
Raglan St. *Glos* —2A **20**
Raikes Rd. *Glos* —5G **19**
Railway Ter. *Ebl* —3G **33**
Raleigh Clo. *C'dwn* —1G **11**
Ramsdale Rd. *Glos* —1E **27**
Rance Pitch. *Upton L* —3F **29**
Randalls Field. *Pain* —6H **31**
(in two parts)
Randolph Clo. *Chel* —3A **16**
Randwick Rd. *Tuf* —3G **27**
Range, The. *H'nam* —4A **8**
Ranmoor. *A'dle* —2E **29**
Ratcliff Lawns. *Sthm* —5G **3**
Ravensgate Rd. *Char K* —5C **16**
Ravis Clo. *Glos* —5C **20**
Reaburn Clo. *Char K* —3C **16**
Read Way. *Bis C* —3E **3**
Rea La. *H'std* —6C **18**
Rectory Ct. *Bis C* —1F **3**
Rectory La. *H'std* —5D **18**
Rectory La. *Swin* —1E **5**
Rectory Rd. *Mat* —1D **28**
Red Admiral Dri. *Abb* —1F **29**
Redding Clo. *Qued* —4B **26**
Reddings Pk. *Red T* —2A **14**
Reddings Rd. *Chel* —2H **13**
Reddings, The. *Chel* —3F **13**
Redgrove Pk. *Chel* —2A **14**
Redgrove Rd. *Chel* —3C **4**
Redhouse La. *Stro* —2G **33**
Redland Clo. *Longl* —5C **10**
Redpoll Way. *A'dle* —5D **20**
Red Rower Clo. *Chel* —2F **5**
Redstart Way. *A'dle* —5D **20**
Redthorne Way. *Up Hat* —4B **14**
Red Well Rd. *Mat* —3C **28**
Redwind Way. *Longl* —4F **11**
Redwood Clo. *Glos* —6G **19**
Redwood Ct. *Chel* —5A **4**
Regent Chambers. *Chel* —6G **5**
Regent Ct. *Chel* —1E **15**
Regent St. *Chel* —6G **5**
Regent St. *Glos* —3H **19**
(in two parts)
Regent St. *S'hse* —4C **32**
Regis Clo. *Char K* —4B **16**
Remus Clo. *Abb* —5G **21**
Rencomb Clo. *Abb* —1F **29**
Reservoir Clo. *Stro* —3F **35**
Reservoir Rd. *Glos* —1H **27**
Reservoir Rd. *Stro* —3F **35**
Retreat, The. *Sel* —6H **33**
Retreat, The. *Tuf* —3G **27**
Ribble Clo. *Brockw* —6E **23**
Richards Rd. *Chel* —3E **5**
Richmond Av. *Glos* —5D **20**
Richmond Dri. *Chel* —6B **6**
Richmond Gdns. *Longl* —4D **10**
Richmonds, The. *A'dle* —1E **29**
Ridgemont Rd. *Stro* —4F **35**
Ridgemount Clo. *Brockw* —6C **22**
Ridings, The. *Mais* —2D **8**
Rippledale Clo. *Chel* —2B **14**
Rissington Clo. *Chel* —1B **14**
Rissington Rd. *Tuf* —3H **27**
Rivelands Rd. *Swin* —6A **2**
River Leys. *Chel* —2C **4**
Rivermead Clo. *Glos* —5H **9**
Riverside Clo. *Chel* —3C **16**
Riversley Rd. *Glos* —1C **20**
Riversmeet. *Brockw* —6E **23**
Riverview Way. *Chel* —3D **4**
Robbers Rd. *Rand* —1F **33**
Robbins Clo. *Ebl* —4F **33**
Robert Burns Av. *Chel* —2A **14**
Robert Raikes Av. *Tuf* —3G **27**
Roberts Clo. *Bis C* —1E **3**
Robertson Rd. *Shur* —1A **24**
Roberts Rd. *Inn* —2F **11**
Roberts Rd. *Pres* —4E **7**
Robin Ct. *S'hse* —2C **32**
Robinhood St. *Glos* —4G **19**
Robins Clo. *Chel* —5B **6**
Robins End. *Inn* —2E **11**
Robinson Rd. *Glos* —4G **19**
Robinswood Gdns. *Glos* —1B **28**
Rochester Clo. *Chel* —4D **14**
Rockleigh Clo. *Tuf* —2H **27**
Rodborough Av. *Stro* —4C **34**
Rodborough Hill. *Stro* —4C **34**
Rodborough La. *Stro* —5D **34**
Rodney Clo. *Longl* —5C **10**
Rodney Rd. *Chel* —6G **5**
Rolleston Way. *Chel* —2C **14**
Roman Hackle Av. *Chel* —2F **5**
Roman Rd. *Abb* —5F **21**
Roman Rd. *Chel* —6D **4**
Roman Way. *Brockw* —5D **22**
Romney Clo. *Glos* —6H **19**
Rookery Rd. *Inn* —3D **10**
Roosevelt Av. *Char K* —1B **16**
Roseberry Av. *Glos* —6H **19**
Rose & Crown Pas. *Chel* —5G **5**
Rosedale Av. *S'hse* —3C **32**
Rosehill Rise. *Chel* —3H **5**
Rosehill St. *Chel* —1A **16**
Rosehip Ct. *Up Hat* —5D **14**
Rosemary Clo. *A'dle* —1D **28**
Rothermere Clo. *Up Hat* —4C **14**
Rothleigh. *Up Hat* —4B **14**
Rotunda Ter. *Chel* —1F **15**
Rowanfield Exchange. *Chel* —5D **4**
Rowanfield Rd. *Chel* —6D **4**
Rowan Gdns. *Brockw* —4C **22**
Rowans, The. *W'cte* —2G **3**
Rowan Way. *Up Hat* —4C **14**
Rowcroft. *Stro* —3C **34**
Rowcroft Retreat. *Stro* —3C **34**
Roxton Dri. *Red T* —2H **13**
Royal Ct. *Chel* —5A **4**
Royal Cres. *Chel* —6G **5**
Royal Oak M. *Chel* —5G **5**
Royal Oak Rd. *Glos* —1G **19**
Royal Pde. Chel —1F **15**
(off Parabola Rd.)
Royal Pde. M. *Chel* —1F **15**
Royal Well La. *Chel* —6G **5**
Royal Well Pl. *Chel* —6G **5**
Royal Well Rd. *Chel* —6G **5**
Rudge, The. *Mais* —1E **9**
Rudhall Ct. Glos —1G **19**
(off Westgate St.)
Rumsey Clo. *A'dle* —1F **29**
Runnings Rd. *Swin* —1D **4**
Runnings, The. *Chel* —1E **5**
Runnymede. *Up Hat* —4B **14**
Rushworth Clo. *Chel* —5A **4**
Rushworth Ho. *Chel* —5A **4**
Rushy Ho. *Chel* —3B **6**
Rushy M. *Chel* —3B **6**
Ruspidge Clo. *Abb* —6F **21**
Russell Pl. *Chel* —4F **5**
Russell St. *Chel* —4F **5**
Russell St. *Glos* —2H **19**
Russell St. *Stro* —3D **34**
Russet Clo. *Tuf* —2E **27**
Russet Rd. *Chel* —4C **4**
Rustic Clo. *Glos* —6D **20**
Rutherford Way. *Swin* —2D **4**
Rydal Rd. *Longl* —5C **10**
Rydal Wlk. *Chel* —2B **14**
Ryder Row. *Inn* —3F **11**
Rye Av. *Chel* —2A **4**
Ryecroft St. *Glos* —3A **20**
Ryeford Ind. Est. *Rye* —4D **32**
Ryeford Rd. (North). *S'hse* —4D **32**
Ryelands. *Tuf* —2F **27**
Ryelands Clo. *S'hse* —2B **32**
Ryelands Rd. *S'hse* —2B **32**
Ryelands, The. *Rand* —1G **33**
Ryeleaze Rd. *Stro* —3D **34**
Ryeworth Dri. *Char K* —2C **16**
Ryeworth Rd. *Char K* —2C **16**

Sackville App. *Chel* —3G **5**
Saddlers Rd. *Qued* —3C **26**
Saffron Clo. *Glos* —6B **20**
Sage Clo. *C'dwn* —3G **11**
St Aidan's Clo. *Chel* —5B **4**
St Alban's Clo. *Chel* —4D **14**
St Albans Rd. *Glos* —6F **19**
St Aldate St. *Glos* —1H **19**
St Aldwyn Rd. *Glos* —5A **20**
St Andrews Grn. *C'dwn* —4A **12**

St Anne's Clo. Brockw —5C 22
St Annes Clo. Chel —5A 6
St Anne's Rd. Chel —6H 5
St Anne's Ter. Chel —6H 5
St Ann Way. Glos —3G 19
St Barnabas Clo. Glos —1H 27
St Brendan's Rd. Stro —3F 35
Saintbridge Clo. Glos —6D 20
Saintbridge Pl. Glos —6C 20
St Catherine St. Glos —6H 9
St Cyrils Rd. S'hse —3C 32
St Davids Clo. Chel —3D 14
St David's Clo. Tuf —2F 27
St Edward's Wlk. Chel —2B 16
St Francis Way. Glos —3E 11
St George's Av. K Stan —6D 32
St Georges Bus. Pk. Chel —5D 4
St George's Clo. Chel —5E 5
St George's Clo. K Stan —6D 32
St George's Clo. Tuf —2F 27
St George's Dri. Chel —5E 5
St George's Pl. Chel —6G 5
St George's Rd. Brockw —6D 22
St George's Rd. Chel —6F 5
St George's Sq. Chel —5G 5
St George's St. Chel —5G 5
St George's Ter. Chel —6F 5
St Giles Ct. Mais —2D 8
St James'. Qued —4C 26
St James Cen., The. Qued —4C 26
St James Clo. Qued —4C 26
St James Pl. Chel —2F 15
St James Sq. Chel —5G 5
St James St. Chel —6H 5
St James St. Glos —3B 20
St John's Av. Chel —6H 5
St John's Av. C'dwn —3H 11
St John's Clo. Bis C —1E 3
St John's La. Glos —1H 19
St Judes Wlk. Chel —3A 16
St Kilda Pde. Glos —2A 20
St Lawrence Rd. Glos —4E 21
St Leonards Clo. Upton L —3F 29
St Luke's Pl. Chel —1H 15
St Luke's Rd. Chel —1H 15
St Luke St. Glos —3G 19
St Margaret's Rd. Chel —5G 5
St Margarets Rd. Huc —3G 21
St Margaret's Ter. Chel —5G 5
St Mark's Ct. Glos —6A 10
St Mark St. Glos —6H 9
St Mary's Clo. Glos —1H 19
St Mary's Sq. Glos —1G 19
St Mary's St. Glos —1H 19
St Mary's St. Pain —5H 31
St Matthews Ct. Stro —4H 33
St Michaels Av. Bis C —2F 3
St Michaels Pl. Stro —2G 33
St Michael's Rd. Chel —3E 15
St Michael's Sq. Glos —2H 19
St Nicholas Ct. Glos —1G 19
(off Archdeacon St.)
St Nicholas Ct. Hard —6B 26
St Nicholas Dri. Chel —2G 5
St Nicholas Sq. Glos —1G 19
St Oswalds Rd. Glos —6G 9
St Paul's Ct. Glos —3H 19
St Paul's La. Chel —4G 5
St Paul's Pde. Chel —5G 5
St Paul's Rd. Chel —4F 5
St Paul's Rd. Glos —3H 19
St Paul's St. N. Chel —5G 5
St Paul's St. S. Chel —5G 5
St Peter's Clo. Chel —3D 4
St Peter's Rd. Mat —2D 28
St Peter's Sq. Chel —3D 4
St Philips Ct. Glos —4G 19
St Phillip's Clo. Huc —3H 21
St Phillip's St. Chel —2G 15
St Stephen's Clo. Chel —2E 15
St Stephen's Rd. Chel —2E 15
St Swithin's. Leon S —6B 32
St Swithuns Rd. H'std —5D 18
St Vincent Way. C'dwn —1H 11
Salamanca Rd. Chel —5C 6
Salisbury Av. Chel —3C 14
Salisbury Rd. Glos —3B 20
Salix Ct. Up Hat —5D 14
Salmons Springs Trad. Est. Stro —1C 34
Salvia Clo. C'dwn —3G 11
Sandalwood Dri. H'std —4E 19
Sandfield Rd. C'dwn —5C 12
Sandford Mill Clo. Chel —2A 16
Sandford Mill Rd. Chel —2A 16
Sandford Pk. Trad. Est. Chel —1H 15
Sandford Rd. Chel —1G 15
Sandford St. Chel —1H 15
Sandford Way. Tuf —4E 27
Sandhurst Rd. Char K —3C 16
Sandhurst Rd. Glos —5H 9
(in two parts)
Sandown Lawn. C'dwn —3H 11
Sandown Rd. Bis C —1E 3
Sandpiper Clo. Qued —4A 26
Sandpits La. Wtrp —1F 33
Sandringham Av. Tuf —4F 27
Sandringham Ct. Chel —2A 16
Sandstar Clo. Longl —4E 11
Sandycroft Rd. C'dwn —2H 11
(in two parts)
Sandy La. Char K —4A 16
Sandy La. Rd. Char K —4A 16
Sandyleaze. Glos —6E 11
Sandy Pluck La. Shur —3G 23
Sappercombe La. Char K —4C 16
Sapperton Rd. Glos —6A 20
Sapphire Clo. Tuf —3E 27
Saturn Clo. Abb —5G 21
Savernake Rd. Glos —4B 20
Saville Clo. Chel —3H 5
Saxon Clo. Longl —4D 10
Saxon Way. Chel —1B 16
Sayers Cres. Brockw —6D 22
Saylittle M. Longl —4F 11
School La. Hard —5A 26
School La. Shur —1B 24
School La. Sthm —5H 3
School Mead. Chel —5D 4
School Rd. Bis C —1F 3
School Rd. Char K —3C 16
School Sq. Sel —6H 33
(off Bell La.)
Scott Av. Glos —1F 27
Scott Ho. Chel —4B 4
Scott Ho. Glos —3G 19
Seabright Clo. Chel —2B 4
Seabroke Rd. Glos —6A 10
Seabrook Rd. Brockw —6D 22
Seacombe Rd. Chel —5A 4
Sebert St. Glos —6A 10
Sedgewick Gdns. Up Hat —3A 14
Sedgley Clo. Tuf —3F 27
Sedgley Rd. Bis C —1E 3
Sefton Wlk. Up Hat —3A 14
Selbourne Rd. Bis C —1E 3
Selkirk Clo. Chel —5A 6
Selkirk Ct. Chel —5A 6
Selkirk Gdns. Chel —5A 6
Selkirk St. Chel —5A 6
Sellars Rd. Hard —6A 26
Selsley Hill. Sel —6H 33
Selworthy. Up Hat —4B 14
Selwyn Clo. Rye —5D 32
Selwyn Rd. Glos —6A 20
Seneca Way. Chel —2E 5
Serlo Rd. Glos —6H 9
Sevelm. Up Hat —4B 14
Seven Posts All. Pres —3C 6
Seventh Av. Tuf —3G 27
Seven Waters. Leon S —6A 32
Severn Clo. Mais —2E 9
Severn Oaks. Qued —6C 26
Severn Rd. Chel —5B 6
Severn Rd. Glos —2G 19
Severn Rd. S'hse —2B 32
Severnside Trad. Est. H'std —2F 19
Severnvale Dri. Qued —4B 26
Seymour Rd. Glos —5G 19
Shackleton Clo. C'dwn —4A 12
Shaftesbury Ind. Est. Chel —1E 5
Shaftesbury Pl. Chel —5A 4
(off Marsland Rd.)
Shakespeare Av. Glos —1F 27
Shakespeare Rd. Chel —5B 4
Shambles, The. Stro —3D 34
Shamrock Clo. C'dwn —3G 11
Shaw Grn. La. Pres —2C 6
Shearwater Gro. Inn —3E 11
Sheepscombe Clo. Chel —1B 14
Sheevaun Clo. Longl —4E 11
Shelburne Rd. Chel —2C 14
Shelley Av. Chel —6B 4
Shelley Av. Glos —1F 27
Shelley Rd. Chel —6B 4
Shepherd Rd. Glos —2E 27
Shepherds Clo. Chel —3A 4
Shepherds Clo. Stro —2E 35
Shepherds Croft. Stro —2E 35
Shepherds Way. C'dwn —2G 11
Sherborne Clo. S'hse —2C 32
Sherborne Ho. S'hse —2C 32
Sherborne Pl. Chel —6H 5
Sherborne St. Chel —5H 5
Sherborne St. Glos —6A 10
Shergar Clo. A'dle —1E 29
Sherwood Grn. Long —3A 10
Shipway Ct. Bis C —1E 3
Short St. Chel —3F 15
Shrublands. Char K —4A 16
Shurdington Rd. Brockw & Shur —6E 23
Shurdington Rd. Chel —5C 14
Sidney St. Chel —6H 5
Sidney St. Glos —2B 20
Silcock Clo. C'dwn —2G 11
Silver Birch Clo. Qued —4B 26
Silver Clo. Tuf —2F 27
Silverdale Pde. Huc —3G 21
Silverthorn Clo. Chel —4E 15
Silverwood Way. Up Hat —4B 14
Simmonds Rd. Huc —4G 21
Simon Rd. Longl —4D 10
Sims La. Qued —2D 26
Sinclair Rd. Shur —2A 24
Sinope St. Glos —2A 20
Sissinghurst Gro. Up Hat —4D 14
Sisson End. Glos —1E 21
Sisson Rd. Glos —1D 20
Sivell Clo. Glos —3B 10
Six Acres. Upton L —2G 29
Skillicorne M. Chel —1D 14
Skinner St. Glos —6H 9
Skylark Way. A'dle —6C 20
Slade Brook. Stro —2F 35
Slad La. Stro —2G 35
Slad Rd. Stro —3D 34
Slaney St. Glos —4A 20
Slimbridge Rd. Tuf —2G 27
Smithwood Gro. Char K —5B 16
Smythe Rd. Swin —1E 5
Snead Pk. Abb —6G 21
Sneedhams Rd. Mat —3C 28
Snowdon Gdns. C'dwn —2H 11
Snowdrop Clo. Abb —6F 21
Snowshill Clo. Barn —4E 21
Snowshill Dri. Barn —4F 21
Snowshill Dri. Bis C —2D 2
Sochi Ct. Chel —5B 4
Solway Rd. Chel —4A 4
Somergate Rd. Chel —3A 4
Somerset Av. Chel —5D 4
Somerset Pl. Glos —3G 19
Somme Rd. Chel —5C 6
Sorrel Clo. Glos —1B 28
Southam La. Sthm —5E 3
Southam Rd. Pres —1D 6
Southbrook Rd. Glos —2D 20
South Clo. Longl —5C 10
Southcourt Clo. Chel —4G 15
Southcourt Dri. Chel —4G 15
Southern Av. Tuf —1H 27
Southern Rd. Chel —5H 15
Southfield App. Chel —5H 15
Southfield Clo. Chel —5H 15
Southfield Mnr. Pk. Char K —6A 16
Southfield Rise. Chel —5H 15
Southfield Rd. Glos —1H 27
Southgate Cres. Stro —5B 34
Southgate Dri. Chel —2A 16
Southgate Gdns. Stro —5B 34
Southgate St. Glos —3G 19
South View. Ebl —3G 33
S. View Way. Pres —3D 6
Southwood La. Chel —1F 15
Sovereign Ct. Glos —1A 20
Spa Rd. Glos —2G 19
Spartan Clo. Abb —5F 21
Spa Vs. Glos —3H 19
Speedwell Clo. Abb —6F 21
Spencer Clo. Huc —4G 21
Spenser Av. Chel —6B 4
Spenser Rd. Chel —6B 4
Spider La. Stro —4E 35
Spillman's Pitch. Stro —4B 34
Spillman's Rd. Stro —4B 34
Spindles, The. Chel —5E 15
Spinnaker Rd. Glos —3F 19
Spinney Rd. Barn —4F 21
Spinney, The. Chel —3H 5
Spire Way. Barn —3E 21
Spread Eagle Rd. Glos —1H 19
Springbank Clo. Chel —3A 4
Springbank Dri. Chel —4A 4
Springbank Gro. Chel —4A 4
Springbank Rd. Chel —4A 4
Springbank Shopping Cen. Chel —3B 4
(off Springbank Way)
Springbank Way. Chel —3A 4
Springfield. Hard —6B 26
Springfield. Stro —4B 34
Springfield Clo. Red T —2G 13
Springfield Rd. Stro —2G 33
Springfield Rd. Upl —2D 34
Spring La. Pres —1C 6
Spring La. Stro —4D 34
Springwell Gdns. C'dwn —2A 12
Square, The. S'hse —2C 32
Square, The. Stro —2D 34
Squirrel Clo. Qued —6B 26
Stables, The. Pres —3E 7
Staites Orchard. Upton L —2F 29
Stamages La. Pain —6H 31
Stamp's Meadow. Long —4A 10
Stancombe Gro. Up Hat —4D 14
Stanleigh Ter. Mais —2D 8
Stanley Pk. Sel —6H 33
Stanley Pl. Chel —4A 4
Stanley Rd. Bat —1B 16
Stanley Rd. Glos —5H 19
Stanley Ter. Glos —4H 19
Stanley, The. Upton L —4G 29
Stanley View. Dud —5A 34
Stanley Wlk. Upton L —4G 29
Stanmoor. A'dle —2F 29
Stansby Cres. C'dwn —3H 11
Stansted Ho. Glos —1G 19
Stanton Rd. Stro —2H 33
Stantons Dri. Swin —6A 2
Stanton Way. Chel —1B 14
Stanway Rd. Chel —1A 14
Stanway Rd. Glos —4D 20
Stanwick Cres. Chel —2E 5
Stanwick Dri. Chel —2E 5
Stanwick Gdns. Chel —3E 5
Starling Ct. S'hse —2C 32
Station App. Glos —1A 20
Station Clo. C'dwn —4C 12
Station Rd. Bis C —1E 3
Station Rd. C'dwn —5B 12
Station Rd. Glos —1H 19
Station Rd. Stro —3C 34
Station St. Chel —5F 5
Station View. Olde —2A 32
Staunton Clo. Abb —1F 29
Steadings Bus. Cen., The. Mais —1D 8
Steeple Clo. Barn —3F 21
Stella Way. Bis C —1C 2
Stepping Stone La. Pain —6G 31
Sterling Ct. Chel —5E 5
Stevans Clo. Long —4B 10
Stewarts Mill La. Abb —1F 29
Stirling Way. Tuf —3E 27
Stirrup, The. Stro —3G 33
Stockley Way. Upton L —6E 29
Stockton Clo. Char K —5A 16
Stockwell La. W'cte —2H 3
Stoke Orchard Rd. Bis C —1A 2
Stoke Rd. Bis C —1C 2
(in two parts)
Stonechat Av. A'dle —6D 20
Stone Clo. Barn —4F 21
Stonecroft Clo. Bis C —1D 2
Stonedale Rd. S'hse —2A 32
Stonehenge Rd. Glos —4C 20
Stonehouse Commercial Cen. S'hse —3A 32
Stoneleigh Clo. Chel —6G 15
Stone Manor. Stro —3F 35
Stoneville St. Chel —5F 5
Stoney Field. H'nam —4B 8
Storrington Pl. S'hse —3C 32
Storrington Rd. S'hse —3C 32
Stow Ct. Chel —6D 4
Stowell M. Barn —4E 21
Strachans Clo. Stro —3B 34
Strand, The. Chel —6H 5
Stratford Clo. Glos —1F 27
Stratford Ct. Stro —3C 34
Stratford Rd. Stro —2A 34
Stratton Rd. Glos —3A 20
Streamside. Bis C —1E 3
Streamside. Stro —3D 34
Street, The. Leon S —6B 32
Strickland Rd. Chel —1A 16
Stringer's Clo. Stro —5B 34
Stringer's Dri. Stro —5B 34
Stroud Rd. Glos & Tuf —3G 19
Stroud Rd. Pain —6G 31
Stroudwater Bus. Pk. S'hse —3A 32
Studland Dri. Pres —3D 6
Stump La. Huc —2B 22
Sudbrook Trad. Est. Glos —3G 19
Sudbrook Way. Glos —6C 20
Sudgrove Pk. Abb —6F 21
Sudmeadow Rd. H'std —1E 19
Suffolk Ho. Chel —1F 15

Suffolk M. *Chel* —1G **15**
Suffolk Pde. *Chel* —1G **15**
Suffolk Pl. *Chel* —1F **15**
Suffolk Rd. *Chel* —2F **15**
Suffolk Sq. *Chel* —1F **15**
Suffolk St. *Chel* —2G **15**
Sulgrave Clo. *Tuf* —4F **27**
Summer Clo. *Stro* —3F **35**
Summer Cres. *Stro* —3F **35**
Summerfield Clo. *Chel* —2C **4**
Summerland Dri. *C'dwn* —4B **12**
Summer St. *Stro* —3E **35**
Sunderland Ct. *C'dwn* —4B **12**
Sunnycroft. *Glos* —6H **19**
Sunnycroft Clo. *Bis C* —2F **3**
Sunnyfield La. *Up Hat* —4H **13**
Sunnyfield Rd. *Hard* —5A **26**
Sunnyhill. *Stro* —2G **33**
(in three parts)
Sunset La. *Sthm* —5H **3**
Sun St. *Chel* —4F **5**
Surrey Av. *Chel* —5C **4**
Sussex Av. *Chel* —5D **4**
Sussex Gdns. *Huc* —4A **22**
Sutton Gdns. *Stro* —3E **35**
Swallow Cres. *Inn* —2E **11**
Swallowtail Clo. *Chel* —5A **4**
Swan Ct. *Glos* —1G **19**
Swan La. *Stro* —3D **34**
Swan Rd. *Glos* —6A **10**
Swanscombe Pl. *Up Hat* —4B **14**
Swanswell Dri. *Chel* —1B **14**
Sweetbriar Clo. *Bis C* —1D **2**
Sweetbriar Houses. *C'dwn* —5C **12**
Sweetbriar St. *Glos* —6H **9**
Swift Rd. *A'dle* —6E **21**
Swifts Hill View. *Stro* —1F **35**
Swindon Clo. *Chel* —4F **5**
Swindon La. *Swin & Chel* —1E **5**
Swindon Pl. *Chel* —5F **5**
Swindon Rd. *Chel* —2E **5**
Swindon St. *Chel* —4F **5**
Swordfish Clo. *C'dwn* —4B **12**
Sybil Rd. *Glos* —5A **20**
Sycamore Clo. *Glos* —6G **19**
Sycamore Ct. *Chel* —5A **4**
Sycamore Dri. *Stro* —2E **35**
Sydenham Rd. N. *Chel* —6A **6**
Sydenham Rd. S. *Chel* —1A **16**
Sydenham Ter. *Glos* —4H **19**
Sydenham Vs. Rd. *Chel* —1A **16**
Sydney. *S'hse* —1B **32**
Synagogue La. *Chel* —6G **5**

Tabernacle Wlk. *Rod* —6B **34**
Tainmor Clo. *Longl* —4F **11**
Talbot M. *Glos* —5G **19**
Talbot Rd. *Chel* —1D **14**
Tall Elms Clo. *C'dwn* —4A **12**
Tallis Rd. *C'dwn* —1G **11**
Tamarisk Ct. *Chel* —5D **14**
Tamarisk M. Qued —4B **26**
(off Azalea Gdns.)
Tamar Rd. *Brockw* —6E **23**
Tamar Rd. *Chel* —5B **6**
Tandey Wlk. *Inn* —3F **11**
Tanners Clo. *Brockw* —5D **22**
Tanners La. *Chel* —4C **4**
Tanner's Rd. *Chel* —4C **4**
Tannery Clo. *Leon S* —6B **32**
Tansy Clo. *Abb* —6G **21**
Target Clo. *Stro* —3G **35**
Tarlton Clo. *Abb* —1F **29**
Tarrington Rd. *Glos* —4A **20**
Tatchley La. *Pres* —3C **6**
Taurus Clo. *Long* —4A **10**
Tayberry Gro. *Up Hat* —5C **14**
Taylors End. *Chel* —3E **15**
Taylors Ground. *Qued* —3C **26**
Teal Clo. *Qued* —4A **26**
Teasel Clo. *Long* —4A **10**
Tebbit M. *Chel* —5H **5**
Teddington Gdns. *Glos* —5C **20**
Telford Ho. *Chel* —4C **4**
Teme Rd. *Chel* —6B **6**
Temple Clo. *Barn* —3F **21**
Tennyson Av. *Glos* —1F **27**
Tennyson Rd. *Chel* —6B **4**
Tensing Rd. *Chel* —5H **15**
Tern Clo. *A'dle* —5D **20**
Terry Ruck Clo. *Chel* —5A **4**
Tetbury Rd. *Tuf* —4H **27**
Tewkesbury Rd. *Elm H* —1A **4**
Tewkesbury Rd. *Glos* —5A **10**
Thames Rd. *Chel* —5B **6**
Thatcher's End. *W'cte* —2G **3**
Theresa St. *Glos* —4G **19**
(in two parts)
Theyer Clo. *Brockw* —6D **22**
Thirlestaine Ho. Cotts. *Chel* —2G **15**
Thirlestaine Rd. *Chel* —2G **15**
Thirlmere Rd. *Chel* —2B **14**
Thistledown Clo. *Chel* —3A **4**
Thomas Moore Clo. *C'dwn* —1H **11**
Thomas Stock Gdns. *Abb* —5F **21**
Thomas St. *Glos* —3A **20**
Thomond Clo. *Chel* —2F **5**
Thompson Dri. *Chel* —5G **15**
Thompson Rd. *Stro* —2E **35**
Thompson Way. *Inn* —3E **11**
Thoresby Av. *Tuf* —4F **27**
Thornbury Clo. *Chel* —5E **5**
Thorncliffe Dri. *Chel* —1E **15**
Thornhaugh M. *Up Hat* —4B **14**
Thornhill Clo. *Glos* —6F **19**
Threadneedle St. *Stro* —3D **34**
Three Cocks La. *Glos* —1G **19**
Three Sisters La. *Pres* —4E **7**
Thrupp La. *Bow* —5F **35**
Thrush Clo. *A'dle* —5D **20**
Tibberton Gro. *Red T* —2G **13**
Tibbiwell. *Pain* —5H **31**
Tibbiwell Gdns. *Pain* —5H **31**
Tibbiwell La. *Pain* —5H **31**
Ticklestone La. *Pain* —6H **31**
Tidswell Clo. *Qued* —5C **26**
Tilney Rd. *Chel* —3G **5**
Timbercombe La. *Char K* —6C **16**
Timbercombe M. *Char K* —5C **16**
Timmis Clo. *Glos* —1D **28**
Timperley Way. *Up Hat* —4B **14**
Tintern Rd. *Tuf* —2G **27**
Tirley Clo. *Qued* —4B **26**
Tiverton Clo. *Chel* —4A **4**
Tivoli Cir. *Chel* —1F **15**
Tivoli La. *Chel* —2F **15**
Tivoli M. *Chel* —1F **15**
Tivoli Rd. *Chel* —2F **15**
Tivoli St. *Chel* —2F **15**
Tivoli Wlk. *Chel* —1E **15**
Tobyfield Clo. *Bis C* —2F **3**
Tobyfield La. *Bis C* —2E **3**
Tobyfield Rd. *Bis C* —1F **3**
Tommy Taylor's La. *Chel* —3G **5**
Tom Price Clo. *Chel* —6H **5**
Tone Dri. *Brockw* —6E **23**
Tower Clo. *Barn* —3E **21**
Townsend St. *Chel* —4F **5**
Trafalgar Dri. *C'dwn* —1G **11**
Trafalgar St. *Chel* —1G **15**
Trajan Clo. *Abb* —5G **21**
Tredworth Rd. *Glos* —4H **19**
Treelands Clo. *Chel* —4G **15**
Treelands Dri. *Chel* —4G **15**
Trent Rd. *Brockw* —6E **23**
Trevor Rd. *Huc* —5G **21**
Triangle, The. *Longl* —6D **10**
Tribune Pl. *Abb* —5F **21**
Trier Way. *Glos* —3G **19**
Trigg Dri. *Stro* —2H **33**
Trinity La. *Chel* —5H **5**
Trinity Rd. *Stro* —4E **35**
Trinity School La. *Chel* —5H **5**
Trowscoed Av. *Chel* —3G **15**
Trubshaw Ct. *C'dwn* —4B **12**
Tryes Rd. *Chel* —3F **15**
Tudor Ct. *Glos* —6B **10**
Tudor Ct. *Leon S* —6B **32**
Tudor Lodge Dri. *Chel* —2F **15**
Tudor Lodge Rd. *Chel* —3F **15**
Tudor St. *Glos* —5F **19**
Tuffley Av. *Glos* —5F **19**
Tuffley Cres. *Glos* —6F **19**
Tuffley La. *Tuf* —2E **27**
Tuffley Trad. Est. *Glos* —1E **27**
Tulworths, The. *Glos* —4C **10**
Tunacre. *H'nam* —4A **8**
Turkdean Rd. *Chel* —1B **14**
Turners Clo. *H'nam* —5A **8**
Tweenbrook Av. *Glos* —5H **19**
Two Hedges Rd. *Bis C* —2E **3**
Twyver Bank. *Upton L* —2G **29**
Twyver Clo. *Upton L* —2G **29**
Tylea Clo. *Red T* —2H **13**
Tyndale Rd. *Huc* —3H **21**
Tynings Ct. *C'dwn* —4C **12**

Ullenwood Rd. *Glos* —4E **21**
Ullswater Rd. *Chel* —2B **14**
Undercliff Av. *Chel* —6G **15**
Undercliff Ter. *Chel* —6G **15**
Underhill Rd. *Mat* —1D **28**
Union St. *Chel* —5H **5**
Union St. *Glos* —6A **10**
Union St. *Stro* —3D **34**
Unwin Clo. *Chel* —2H **13**
Unwin Rd. *Chel* —2H **13**
Uphill Pl. *Glos* —6G **19**
Uplands Rd. *Stro* —2D **34**
Up. Bath St. *Chel* —2G **15**
Up. Church Rd. *Stro* —3H **33**
Up. Dorrington Ter. *Stro* —4E **35**
Upperfield Rd. *King T* —2D **4**
Up. Hatherley Way. *Up Hat* —3A **14**
Up. Leazes. *Stro* —3E **35**
Up. Mill La. *Pres* —2E **7**
Up. Mills Ind. Est. *S'hse* —4C **32**
Up. Norwood St. *Chel* —3F **15**
Up. Park St. *Chel* —1A **16**
Up. Quay St. *Glos* —1G **19**
Up. Queens Rd. *S'hse* —3C **32**
Up. Springfield Rd. *Upl* —2D **34**
Up. Tynings. *C Grn* —2G **33**
Up. Washwell. *Pain* —4H **31**
Upton Clo. *Barn* —4F **21**
Upton Hill. *Upton L* —5E **29**
Upton La. *Abb* —6G **21**
Upton St. *Glos* —3A **20**
Usk Way. *Brockw* —6E **23**

Valerian Clo. *Abb* —4F **21**
Valley Cotts. *Upton L* —4H **29**
Valley La. *Upton L* —4H **29**
Valley View Rd. *Stro* —4F **35**
Vatch View. *Stro* —1F **35**
Vauxhall Rd. *Glos* —3A **20**
Vauxhall Ter. *Glos* —2A **20**
Vensfield Rd. *Qued* —3B **26**
Verbena Clo. *Abb* —6F **21**
Vernal Clo. *Abb* —6G **21**
Verney Clo. *Chel* —3H **15**
Verney Rd. *S'hse* —3C **32**
Verneys, The. *Chel* —3H **15**
Vernon Pl. *Chel* —6H **5**
Vertican Rd. *Inn* —3E **11**
Vervain Clo. *C'dwn* —2H **11**
Vetch Clo. *Glos* —1B **28**
Viburnum View. *Abb* —6G **21**
Vicarage Clo. *C'dwn* —5B **12**
Vicarage Clo. *Shur* —1B **24**
Vicarage Ct. *Brockw* —6D **22**
Vicarage La. *Brockw* —6D **22**
Vicarage Rd. *Glos* —4B **20**
Vicarage St. *Pain* —5H **31**
Victoria Ct. *Long* —3A **10**
Victoria Pl. *Chel* —6A **6**
Victoria Retreat. *Chel* —2G **15**
Victoria Rd. *Long* —3A **10**
Victoria St. *Chel* —4G **5**
Victoria St. *Glos* —3A **20**
Victoria St. *Pain* —5H **31**
Victoria Ter. *Chel* —6A **6**
Victory Clo. *C'dwn* —1H **11**
Victory Rd. *Glos* —4A **20**
Vigar Rd. *Hard* —6A **26**
Village Rd. *Chel* —3C **4**
Vilverie Mead. *Bis C* —1C **2**
Vincent Av. *Tuf* —4F **27**
Vine Ct. *Chel* —4F **5**
Vineries Clo. *Chel* —5F **15**
Vines, The. *Huc* —4A **22**
Vine Ter. *Glos* —6A **10**
Vineyard La. *Chel* —5D **4**
Vineyards Clo. *Char K* —5C **16**
Vittoria Wlk. *Chel* —1G **15**
Voxwell La. *Bis C* —2D **2**
Voyce Clo. *Tuf* —3G **27**
Vulcan Way. *Abb* —5G **21**

Waldrist Clo. *Chel* —2C **4**
Walham La. *Glos* —5G **9**
Walkley Hill. *Stro* —5B **34**
Wallbridge. *Stro* —3C **34**
Waller Dri. *Barn* —3F **21**
Walnut Clo. *A'dle* —2E **29**
Walnut Clo. *Chel* —3H **5**
Walton Clo. *Upton L* —2F **29**
Ward Av. *Inn* —3E **11**
Ward Clo. *Bis C* —1F **3**
Warden Hill Clo. *Chel* —3C **14**
Warden Hill Rd. *Chel* —3C **14**
Wards Rd. *Chel* —3A **14**
Warren Clo. *Chel* —3C **14**
Warren Clo. *C'dwn* —2H **11**
Warwick Av. *Tuf* —4F **27**
Warwick Clo. *Stro* —6B **34**
Warwick Cres. *Char K* —3C **16**
Warwick Pl. *Chel* —5H **5**
Wasley Rd. *Chel* —6B **4**
Waterfield Clo. *Chel* —2G **15**
Water La. *Char K* —3C **16**
Water La. *Sel* —6H **33**
Waterloo St. *Chel* —4E **5**
Watermans Ct. *Qued* —4A **26**
Watermead La. *Brockw* —1D **30**
Water Meadow. *Qued* —6B **26**
Watermoor Clo. *Chel* —3A **4**
Watermoor Ct. *C'dwn* —4A **12**
Watershoot Clo. *Pres* —2B **6**
Waterside Clo. *Qued* —4A **26**
Waters Reach. *H'std* —5E **19**
Water Wheel Clo. *Qued* —4A **26**
Watery La. *Upton L* —5G **29**
Watson Gro. *Abb* —6A **22**
Watts Clo. *Huc* —4A **22**
Waverley Rd. *Glos* —1D **20**
Wayridge, The. *A'dle* —1E **29**
Weald Clo. *Glos* —6D **20**
Weavers Rd. *Qued* —3C **26**
Wedgwood Dri. *Longl* —5D **10**
Weir Bri. Clo. *Glos* —3F **21**
Welch Rd. *Chel* —3B **4**
Welland Ct. *Chel* —3B **6**
Welland Dri. *Chel* —3B **6**
Welland Lodge Rd. *Chel* —3A **6**
Wellbrook Rd. *Bis C* —1E **3**
Well Cross Rd. *Glos* —1A **28**
Well End. *Stro* —1F **35**
Well End Rd. *Qued* —3C **26**
Weller Bungalows. *Glos* —1F **27**
Wellesley Rd. *Chel* —4G **5**
(in two parts)
Wellesley St. *Glos* —5A **20**
Wellington La. *Chel* —5H **5**
Wellington Pde. *Glos* —1A **20**
Wellington Rd. *Chel* —4H **5**
Wellington Sq. *Chel* —4H **5**
Wellington St. *Chel* —6G **5**
Wellington St. *Glos* —2H **19**
Well Pl. *Chel* —6E **5**
Wells Clo. *Chel* —4C **14**
Wellsprings Rd. *Glos* —6D **10**
Wells Rd. *Glos* —2D **20**
Well Wlk. *Chel* —5G **5**
Welveland La. *Barn* —2F **21**
Welwyn M. *Up Hat* —4B **14**
Wendover Gdns. *Chel* —6E **5**
Wentworth Clo. *Chel* —4A **4**
Wentworth Clo. *Glos* —4C **10**
Wentworth Rd. *Chel* —4A **4**
Wesley Ct. *Glos* —2A **20**
Wesley Ct. *Stro* —3D **34**
Wesley Rd. *Leon S* —6B **32**
Wessex Dri. *Chel* —6C **6**
Westal Grn. *Chel* —1E **15**
Westal Pk. *Chel* —2E **15**
West App. Dri. *Chel* —3H **5**
Westbourne Dri. *Chel* —5A **6**
Westbourne Dri. *Hard* —6B **26**
Westbury Rd. *Chel* —4H **15**
Westbury Rd. *Tuf* —2G **27**
Westcote Rd. *Tuf* —4H **27**
Westdown Gdns. *Chel* —6A **6**
West Dri. *Chel* —4H **5**
West End La. *Huc* —5A **22**
Westend Pde. *Glos* —6F **9**
Westend Ter. *Glos* —6F **9**
Western Ct. *Chel* —6E **5**
Western Rd. *Chel* —6E **5**
West Field. *H'nam* —4A **8**
Westfield Av. *Brockw* —5C **22**
Westfield Rd. *Brockw* —5C **22**
Westfield Ter. *Long* —4H **9**
Westgate Galleria, The. *Glos* —6G **9**
Westgate St. *Glos* —1G **19**
Westland Rd. *Hard* —6A **26**
W. Lodge Dri. *Glos* —4E **21**
Westmead Rd. *Longl* —4E **11**
Westminster Clo. *Chel* —2A **16**
Westminster Ct. *Glos* —1C **20**
Weston Rd. *Glos* —3G **19**
Westover Ct. *C'dwn* —2A **12**
Westrip La. *Stro* —2G **33**
Westrip Pl. *Stro* —2G **33**
Westward Ct. *Ebl* —4G **33**
Westward Rd. *Ebl* —4F **33**
Westwood La. *Pres* —4E **7**
Wetherleigh Dri. *H'nam* —4B **8**
Weyhouse Clo. *Stro* —5E **35**
Whaddon Av. *Chel* —5B **6**
Whaddon Dri. *Chel* —5A **6**
Whaddon Rd. *Chel* —5A **6**
Whaddon Way. *Tuf* —4G **27**
Wharfdale Way. *S'hse* —4B **32**

Wheatland Dri. *Chel* —3A **4**
Wheatridge Ct. *A'dle* —6E **21**
Wheatridge E., The. *A'dle* —1F **29**
Wheatridge, The. *A'dle* —1E **29**
Wheatsheaf Dri. *Bis C* —1C **2**
Wheatstone Rd. *Glos* —4H **19**
Wheatway. *A'dle* —2E **29**
Wheelers Wlk. *Stro* —2A **34**
Whitcomb Clo. *Upton L* —3F **29**
Whitebeam Clo. *Glos* —4C **10**
Whitecross Sq. *Chel* —2H **15**
Whitefield Clo. *S'hse* —4C **32**
Whitehall. *Stro* —3E **35**
Whitehart St. *Chel* —4F **5**
Whitehorse La. *Pain* —5H **31**
Whitehouse Pk. *Cain* —3H **33**
Whitehouse Way. *W'cte* —2G **3**
Whitemarsh Clo. *Chel* —3A **4**
Whitethorn Dri. *Pres* —4C **6**
Whiteway Rd. *Mat* —6C **20**
Whitewell Clo. *Barn* —4F **21**
Whitfield St. *Glos* —2H **19**
Whittington Rd. *Chel* —1A **14**
Whittle Av. *Tuf* —4G **27**
Whittle Clo. *Chel* —1H **13**
Whitworth M. *Huc* —5B **22**
Whornes Orchard. *Upton L* —2G **29**
Wickridge Clo. *Stro* —2E **35**
Wicliffe Ind. Cen. *Stro* —4B **34**
Widden St. *Glos* —2A **20**
Wigmore Clo. *Abb* —5F **21**
Wilkes Av. *Huc* —3H **21**
Willcox Dri. *W'cte* —2G **3**
Willersey Rd. *Chel* —1B **14**
William Gough Clo. *Chel* —2A **4**
Williams Orchard. *H'nam* —4A **8**
Willow Av. *Glos* —4C **20**
Willowbrook Dri. *Chel* —3A **4**
Willow Clo. *W'cte* —2G **3**
Willowcroft Clo. *Mat* —2E **29**
Willowherb Clo. *Pres* —4D **6**
Willowleaze. *Glos* —6E **11**
Willow Pk. Dri. *Bis C* —1E **3**
Willow Rd. *Char K* —4D **16**
Willow Rd. *Chel* —6C **6**
Willow Rd. *K Stan* —6D **32**
Willow Rd. *S'hse* —3B **32**
Willows, The. *Glos* —6A **10**
Willows, The. *Qued* —4B **26**
Willow Way. *Glos* —4C **20**
Wilson Rd. *Shur* —2A **24**
Wilton Clo. *Glos* —5G **19**
Wilton Rd. *Glos* —5G **19**
Wimborne Clo. *Up Hat* —3B **14**
Winchcombe Rd. *Tuf* —3H **27**
Winchcombe St. *Chel* —6H **5**
(in three parts)
Winchester Dri. *Tuf* —2H **27**
Winchester Way. *Chel* —3C **14**
Windermere Clo. *Chel* —2B **14**
Windermere Rd. *Chel* —2B **14**
Windermere Rd. *Glos* —5D **10**
Windrush Rd. *Chel* —5B **6**
Windrush Rd. *Tuf* —3H **27**
Windsor Dri. *Tuf* —3F **27**
Windsor St. *Chel* —4A **6**
Windyridge Gdns. *Chel* —2F **5**
Windyridge Rd. *Chel* —3E **5**
Winnycroft La. *Mat* —5C **28**
Winsley Rd. *Mat* —1D **28**
Winslow Pl. *C'dwn* —3A **12**
Winstonian Rd. *Chel* —5A **6**
Winston Rd. *C'dwn* —4A **12**
Winterbotham Rd. *Chel* —4A **4**
Winton Clo. *Chel* —2C **14**
Winton Rd. *Chel* —2D **14**
Wishford Clo. *Longl* —5F **11**
Wisteria Ct. *Up Hat* —5D **14**
Wisteria Way. *C'dwn* —3H **11**
Wistley Rd. *Char K* —5C **16**
Witcombe Pl. *Chel* —6H **5**
Withers, The. *Bis C* —1D **2**
Withyfield Rd. *Bis C* —1F **3**
Withyholt Ct. *Char K* —4A **16**
Withyholt Pk. *Char K* —4A **16**
Withy M. *Glos* —6C **20**
Withypool. *Up Hat* —4B **14**
Witley Lodge Clo. *Up Hat* —3A **14**
Woburn Av. *Tuf* —4F **27**
Wolseley Rd. *Glos* —1D **20**
Wolseley Ter. *Chel* —1G **15**
Woodbine Clo. *Abb* —6F **21**
Woodborough Clo. *Pain* —6H **31**
Woodcock Clo. *A'dle* —6D **20**
Woodcock Clo. *S'hse* —1C **32**
Woodcock La. *S'hse* —2C **32**
Woodcote. *Glos* —4C **10**
Woodend Clo. *Barn* —3F **21**
Woodford Ct. *Glos* —4C **20**
Woodgate Clo. *Barn* —4F **21**
Woodgate Clo. *Char K* —4D **16**
Woodhouse Dri. *Stro* —4C **34**
Woodland Grn. *Upton L* —2F **29**
Woodlands Dri. *Stro* —2F **35**
Woodlands Pk. Cvn. Pk. *Qued* —4A **26**
Woodlands Rd. *Chel* —4E **15**
Woodlands, The. *Leon S* —6B **32**
Woodlands, The. *Stro* —2E **35**
Woodleigh Field. *H'nam* —4B **8**
Woodmancote Vale. *W'cte* —1G **3**
Woodmans Way. *Bis C* —2E **3**
Woodpecker Rd. *Pod* —6F **19**
Woodrow Way. *Glos* —2D **26**
Woodruff Clo. *Glos* —1C **28**
Woodside. *Stro* —2G **35**
Woods Orchard. *Tuf* —3A **28**
Woods Orchard Rd. *Tuf* —3H **27**
Wood Stanway Dri. *Bis C* —1D **2**
Woolstrop Ho. *Qued* —4C **26**
Woolstrop Way. *Qued* —2D **26**
Worcester Pde. *Glos* —6H **9**
Worcester St. *Chel* —3E **5**
Worcester St. *Glos* —1H **19**
Wordens, The. *Stro* —2G **33**
Wordsworth Av. *Chel* —6B **4**
Wotton Ct. *Barn* —2E **21**
Wotton Elms Ct. *Glos* —1C **20**
Wotton Hill. *Glos* —1B **20**
Wren Clo. *A'dle* —5C **20**
Wren Ter. *Inn* —3E **11**
Wychbury Clo. *Chel* —4G **15**
Wye Rd. *Brockw* —6E **23**
Wymans Ct. *Chel* —2F **5**
Wymans La. *Swin* —2E **5**
Wyman's Rd. *Chel* —4B **6**

Yarlington Clo. Bis C —1D 2
(off Lyndley Chase)
Yarnolds. *Shur* —2A **24**
Yarnold Ter. *Chel* —3D **4**
Yarrow Clo. *Glos* —1B **28**
Yeend Clo. *Chel* —2C **4**
Yew Tree Clo. *Chel* —2F **5**
Yew Tree Way. *C'dwn* —4G **11**
York Rd. *Glos* —3D **20**
York Row. *Chel* —3B **6**
York St. *Chel* —5H **5**
York Ter. *Chel* —6F **5**

Zinnia Clo. *C'dwn* —2G **11**
Zoons Rd. *Huc* —3H **21**

INDEX TO PLACES OF INTEREST

with their map square reference

*Bishop Hooper Memorial. —1G **19***
(off St Mary's Sq.)
*Blackfriars. —2G **19***
(off Blackfriars)
Buckholt Wood Nature Reserve. —6D **30**

Cheltenham Art Gallery & Museum. —5G **5**
Cheltenham College. —2G **15**
Cheltenham Racecourse. —1B **6**
Cheltenham Tourist Info. Cen. —6G **5**
Crickley Hill Country Park. —6C **24**

Devil's Chimney. —2G **25**

Folk Museum. —1G **19**

Gloucester Cathedral. —1H **19**
Gloucester City Library, Museum & Art —2H **19**
Gloucester Tourist Info. Cen. —2H **19**
Great Witcombe Roman Villa. (Remains of) —4E **31**
*Greyfriars. —2H **19***
(off Greyfriars)

Hall of Fame. —1H **5**
Holst Birthplace Museum. —5H **5**
House of the Tailor of Gloucester. —1H **19**

Lineover Wood Nature Reserve. —6G **17**
*Little Fleece Bookshop. —5H **31***
(off New St.)
Llanthony Priory. (Remains of) —3F **19**

National Waterways Museum. —2G **19**

Over Bridge. —5E **9**

Pittville Pump Room. (Spa) —3H **5**
Prinknash Abbey. —5A **30**
Prinknash Bird Park. —6A **30**
Prison Museum. —1G **19**

Robert Opie Collection. —2G **19**
Robins Wood Hill Country Park. —2A **28**
Robins Wood Visitors Cen. —1A **28**
Rodborough Common. —6C **34**

St Oswalds Priory. —6H **9**
Selsley Herb Garden. —6H **33**
Soldiers of Gloucestershire Museum. —2G **19**
Stroud District Museum. —3D **34**
Stroud Pottery. —5B **30**
Stroud Tourist Info. Cen. —3D **34**

Transport Museum. —1G **19**

Witcombe Reservoirs Nature Reserve. —2F **31**

Every possible care has been taken to ensure that the information given in this publication is accurate and whilst the publishers would be grateful to learn of any errors, they regret they cannot accept any responsibility for loss thereby caused.

The representation on the maps of a road, track or footpath is no evidence of the existence of a right of way.

The Grid on this map is the National Grid taken from the Ordnance Survey map with the permission of the Controller of Her Majesty's Stationery Office.